NOT BY

SIGHT

"Vivid, nourishing sketches of Bible characters learning to live with their some-times startling Lord."

J. I. Packer, Board of Governors' Professor of Theology, Regent College

"To live by faith is no small thing. Jon Bloom's *Not by Sight* provides brief read-ings—one per day would be ideal—to help us rethink our lives in the light of Christ's faithfulness. The audacity of this book is that it simply but thoughtfully takes Christ at his word. How rare, how powerful."

Ray Ortlund, Immanuel Church, Nashville

"Spurgeon said, 'My books are my tools.' And the book you hold in your hands is one wise match for the journey. Bloom's stories and insights ignite—ignite fire in bones, and ignite the old and best paths, and ignite glimpses of God's glory that make us want to run this walk of faith!"

Ann Voskamp, author, *New York Times* bestseller, *One Thousand Gifts: A Dare to Live Fully Right Where You Are*

"Jon Bloom is a Christ-centered, God-worshiping, kingdom-oriented guy. And since not all writers are, those are good reasons to read this book! But it's more than that. Jon is a gifted writer of something we need more of—truth-telling nonfiction that's full of imagination. For years I have read Jon's *Desiring God* blogs and pondered them, saving some of them to quote from in future books. I love how Jon repeatedly takes me back to Scripture. God says his words won't return to him empty without accomplishing his purpose. He never says that about our words. That's why *Not by Sight* will endure beyond this world—it is infused with the life-giving Word of God that will never die."

Randy Alcorn, Eternal Perspective Ministries

"*Not by Sight* creatively and winsomely invites readers into the realities of the Gospel accounts, enabling us to hear the rocks of the adulterous woman's ac-cusers fall to the ground, feel the tingle of health rushing through the leper's body, see the panic in Peter's eyes as he begins to sink, smell the fragrance that has been poured on Jesus's feet, and taste the fish Jesus serves to the disciples for breakfast."

Nancy Guthrie, author of *Hearing Jesus Speak into Your Sorrow* and the Seeing Jesus in the Old Testament series

"Forgetfulness and familiarity. Faith is often plagued by these twin faults. We easily forget what we know about who God is and what he's done for us in Jesus Christ. When we turn to Scripture for help, our familiarity dulls the wonder in the splendid story of God's mercy to mere men. We need to be reminded of the old stories of Scripture, that they might irrigate our parched souls and ignite our faith. In *Not by Sight*, my friend Jon Bloom shatters our familiarity with the Bible by helping us see afresh how the drama of Scripture unfolds in the gritty reality of human experience and how those stores are infused with grace as they fit into the greatest story: God's plan to save sinners by his Son. Do you need to be reminded of what you already know? Do you need to be shaken from your familiarity? Jon's fresh tellings of the old tales will help you recover surprise and delight in the stories of Scripture."

C. J. Mahaney, Sovereign Grace Ministries; author, *Living the Cross Centered Life*

"There is nothing quite like the gritty, grace-filled stories of Scripture to awaken our hearts to the all-sufficiency of Jesus Christ. And there is hardly anyone I know more gifted or capable of bringing them to life and making poignant, and often painful, application of them than my good friend, Jon Bloom. This is a wonderfully insightful, powerfully edifying, and above all Christ-exalting book that I cannot recommend too highly."

Sam Storms, Bridgeway Church, Oklahoma City, Oklahoma

"Do you, like me, feel the futility of straining to get hope from the things you can see? Using the voices of those who have gone before us, Jon Bloom describes the better way—walking by faith with Jesus, our blessed hope. *Not by Sight* takes you on a walk through the cloud of witnesses whose testimony of God's always sufficient grace echoes through the ages. I'm grateful for this meditation on the precious promise of God's provision to enable us to put one foot in front of the other by faith."

Gloria Furman, author, *Glimpses of Grace*

"What happens when we humbly and expectantly meditate on the stories of the Scriptures while wearing the lens of the gospel? Ask Jon Bloom, or better still, buy his new book, *Not by Sight*, and discover for yourself. This treasury of short devotionals is the nourishing fruit of a man smitten with Jesus and hungry for grace—a brother whose words make the gospel beautiful and believable, to believers and nonbelievers alike. This is a book you're going to want to give to a whole lot of friends, no matter where they are in their faith story."

Scotty Smith, Founding Pastor, Christ Community Church, Franklin, Tennessee; author, *The Reign of Grace*, *Restoring Broken Things*, and *Everyday Prayers: 365 Days to a Gospel-Centered Faith*

"There are probably only two books I've read with a depth of discipleship untouched by the church at large in America. *Not by Sight* by Jon Bloom is one of those. More than once, I found myself unable to continue reading as tears filled my eyes, my heart being so deeply moved and encouraged by Jon's soothing words about the surprising but always trustworthy ways of God. More Christians need to understand these truths if they are to walk firmly into every good work God has prepared for them. If you read only one book this year, I strongly recommend it be this one."

Matt Brown, Evangelist; author; Founder, Think Eternity

NOT BY

SIGHT

A FRESH LOOK AT OLD STORIES
OF WALKING BY FAITH

JON BLOOM

FOREWORD BY **JOHN PIPER**

CROSSWAY

WHEATON, ILLINOIS

Not by Sight: A Fresh Look at Old Stories of Walking by Faith

Copyright © 2013 by Desiring God

Published by Crossway
      1300 Crescent Street
      Wheaton, Illinois 60187

Cover design: Josh Dennis

Cover image: Shutterstock and iStock

First printing 2013

Printed in the United States of America

Trade paperback ISBN: 978-1-4335-3593-2
PDF ISBN: 978-1-4335-3594-9
Mobipocket ISBN: 978-1-4335-3595-6
ePub ISBN: 978-1-4335-3596-3

Library of Congress Cataloging-in-Publication Data

Bloom, Jon, 1965–
   Not by sight : a fresh look at old stories of walking by faith / Jon Bloom ; foreword by John Piper.
     p.   cm.
   Includes bibliographical references and index.
   ISBN 978-1-4335-3593-2 (tp)
   1. Trust in God—Christianity—Biblical teaching. 2. Bible stories. I. Title.
BV4637.B56   2013
242'.5—dc23   2012033798

Crossway is a publishing ministry of Good News Publishers.

VP		22	21	20	19	18	17	16	15	14
15	14	13	12	11	10	9	8	7	6	5	4

To Pam

My precious partner in believing God's
"precious and very great promises" (2 Pet. 1:4).
Thank you for helping me more than
anyone else to believe in Jesus,
and for praying more than
anyone else for this little book.

CONTENTS

FOREWORD

JOHN PIPER

WITH THE APOSTLE JOHN I say, *I am writing these things to you so that my joy may be complete* (1 John 1:4). *My* joy. Yes, yours too. But that's not my point yet.

To write on behalf of Jon Bloom and his book is a joy. So indulge me for a moment, if you are willing.

First, I love Jon Bloom. I want to praise the man. He is worthy of your attention.

Jon is a man of worship. He lives under the sovereign grace of God with a happy sense of submission and praise. In fact, he is a worship leader at his church.

Jon is a lover of the gospel of Jesus. He is manifestly glad that his sins are forgiven because of Christ, and his works are the fruit of his justification, not the root.

Jon is humble and ready to confess his sin and heal relationships.

Jon is strong in the Scriptures. He has a backbone and is not easily duped.

Jon is a man of vision—a vision for his life and family, and a vision for Desiring God. He has overseen this ministry since the beginning with far-seeing dreams.

Jon is reliable. I would trust him with my life. Indeed, I have trusted him with the ministry—which is a huge part of my life.

> Jon is wise. Though he is a generation younger than I am, I
> would turn to him before most older men. There is a gift of
> wisdom. Jon has it. He is my counselor.

Not surprisingly, then, this book is also worthy of your attention. All that Jon is as a person is poured out here. And his gifts.

Jon is creative. These meditations are not your ordinary exposition. These are stories. Really good stories. They are rooted in what the Bible says. The creative additions never go beyond what really *could* have happened. The truths that Jon sees for our lives are based not on what might have been but on what was. The might-have-beens give added flesh to the bones of truth. They are touchable.

Jon is persuaded that if you know the truth, the truth will make you free. And truths about the greatness of Christ are the best ones for freeing us from unbelief. And to be freed from unbelief is to be freed from fear and greed and pride and anger and lust and despair and a hundred other permutations of life-ruining sins.

New Christians or old Christians, what we need in order to walk by faith and not by sight is glimpses. I know that sounds contradictory. *We need sight not to walk by sight?* But it's not contradictory, because the sight we need is not a sight of what the day holds, but a sight of who holds the day.

And even that sight happens by looking through the window of the *word*. Which means we see with our ears. Yes, it sounds strange. But listen: "The LORD *revealed himself* to Samuel at Shiloh by the *word* of the LORD" (1 Sam. 3:21). So we "look" through the window of the word with our ears, and what we hear is a sight of God!

If that makes no sense to you, here's a suggestion. Pick a chapter in this book whose title looks relevant for you. Listen as you read. *Look* through what you *hear*. And see if Jesus does not show himself to you in such a way that you trust him more.

That is what Jon Bloom desires. That is what we both are praying for—your joy of faith. So yes, I wrote this for *my* joy. And mine will be full if I hear that my happy commendations and Jon's beautiful narrations awaken in *you* the gladness of walking by faith, *Not by Sight*.

John Piper
Founder and Teacher, Desiring God
Chancellor, Bethlehem College and Seminary

"These are written so that you may believe
that Jesus is the Christ, the Son of God,
and that by believing you
may have life in his name."

John 20:31

A WORD TO
THE READER

WHAT DOES JESUS REALLY want from you? So much needs to be said.[1] But boiled down to one sentence it's this: "Believe in God; believe also in me" (John 14:1). That's why when the apostle John wrote his gospel, he used some form of the word "believe" eighty-five times in twenty-one chapters. What he remembered Jesus emphasizing in his teaching and preaching was *believing*.

Whether or not you believe in Jesus is the most important issue of your life because "whoever believes in the Son has eternal life; whoever does not obey the Son shall not see life, but the wrath of God remains on him" (John 3:36). You see, "without faith it is impossible to please him, for whoever would draw near to God must believe that he exists and that he rewards those who seek him" (Heb. 11:6).

But believing in Jesus is very difficult. It's difficult because "the whole world lies in the power of the evil one" (1 John 5:19), and he works with all his might to blind "the minds of the unbelievers, to keep them from seeing the light of the gospel of the glory of Christ, who is the image of God" (2 Cor. 4:4). And he is constantly trying to lead believers astray (Matt. 24:24).

Because of this, it is crucial that followers of Jesus learn to "walk by faith, not by sight" (2 Cor. 5:7). In other words, we must learn to trust God's promises more than we trust

---

[1] I highly recommend John Piper's book, *What Jesus Demands from the World* (Wheaton, IL: Crossway, 2006).

our perceptions. This theme is woven through the Bible from beginning to end.

The purpose of this little book is to imaginatively reflect on the real experiences of real people in the Bible in order to help you grasp and live what it means to "trust in the Lord with all your heart, and . . . not lean on your own understanding" (Prov. 3:5). Its goal is to help you believe in Jesus while living in a very confusing and painful world.

Jesus said, "This is the work of God, that you believe in him whom he has sent" (John 6:29). My prayer is that God will use this book to encourage you in the most important work you will ever do in your life.

GRATITUDE

IT IS A GIFT beyond comprehension to be married to Pamela, who has walked with me by faith in Jesus since we fell in love as teenagers. No other mortal understands as deeply how desperately meaningful 2 Corinthians 5:7 is to me. And none has helped me more to live it. Pam, "thank you" is packed with the ineffable, and this little book is dedicated to you.

John Piper has been a pastor, teacher, mentor, father, and dear friend to me for over twenty years, and his influence on me is pervasive and unequaled. John, our long partnership at Desiring God is and always will be among the highest privileges of my life. Writing the foreword for this book was one more kindness added to the myriad I have received from you.

This book exists in large part because of the encouragement and help of my incredible colleagues (past and present) at DG, especially John Knight, Carol Steinbach, Bryan DeWire, Joe Scheumann, and Andrea Froehlich who proofed and improved these meditations when they were written as monthly devotionals for DG's supporters. And because Justin Taylor and the Crossway team were willing to get behind it. My gratitude for you all runs deeper than I can express.

But Jesus, my deepest thanks is reserved for you. Since I first trusted you when I was young, you have never broken a single promise, but have faithfully led me in paths of righteousness (Ps. 23:3), the kind that can only be walked by faith (2 Cor. 5:7). Following you on these paths with your Word as my lamp (Ps. 119:105) has been harder than I ever imagined and the sweetest thing I've ever known. In fact, the sweetest things have come from the hardest, darkest, most painful parts of the journey. The sweet and the bitter both make me long for the day when the sight of faith will finally give way to the sight of your face (1 Cor. 13:12). I hope it's soon.

And he awoke and rebuked the wind and the raging waves, and they ceased, and there was a calm. He said to them, "Where is your faith?" And they were afraid.

LUKE 8:24–25

1

"WHERE IS YOUR FAITH?"

JAMES ZEBEDEE AND FEAR

Luke 8:22–25

THE SEA WAS QUIET now. And there was just breeze enough to push the boat along.

The disciples were quiet too. Andrew was steering. He had taken over for Peter, who sat wrapped in a cloak, exhausted and lost in thought. He had been soaked to the skin. A few others were bailing out the remaining water.

Jesus was sleeping again.

James leaned on the bow gunwale watching reflections dance on gentle waves.

James knew this sea. He and John had spent most of their lives on or in it. His father was a fisherman. So were most of his male kin and friends. His memory flashed the faces of some of them who had drowned in unpredictable Galilean windstorms like the one that had pummeled them barely a half hour ago.

A seasoned boatman, James was not alarmed easily. But he knew a man-eater when he saw it. This storm had opened its mouth to swallow them all into the abyss.

Terror had been in John's eyes when he grabbed James and yelled, "We have to tell the Master!" They stumbled to the stern. How Jesus had remained sleeping while the furious surf tossed the boat around was itself a wonder. They woke him screaming, "Master, Master, we are perishing!" (v. 24).

James would never forget the way Jesus looked at him. His eyes were at once potent and tranquil. No trace of fear. Laying aside the blanket, Jesus rose to full height on the rear deck. James, fearing Jesus was about to be pitched overboard, reached to grab him just as Jesus shouted, "Peace! Be still!" (Mark 4:39).

No sooner had those words left his mouth and the wind was completely gone! The sudden hush of the howling was otherworldly. The waves immediately began to abate. Each disciple stood where he was, looking dumbfounded at the water and sky and each other.

Jesus's gaze lingered for a moment on the steep hills along the western shore. Then he looked around at the Twelve and said, "Where is your faith?" (v. 25).

He had looked right at James when he said "faith."

Now, as James leaned on the bow, he turned Jesus's question over and over in his mind.

"Where is your *faith*?" When Jesus first said it, James felt its intended rebuke. Didn't he trust God? He thought he had. But the storm proved that all the confidence he felt when the pressure was off was fair-weather faith. The Galilean westerlies had swept it away. He felt chastened and humbled.

But the more James thought about the question, the deeper it dug into him. "*Where* is your faith?" Where? My faith is in what I see. My faith is in what I feel. When the storm hit, I trusted what my eyes saw. I trusted what my skin felt. I trusted the violent force that was tossing the boat like a toy. I trusted the stories told by my father. I trusted the tragedies I remember. I trusted the power of the storm because storms kill people.

Is that wrong? Up until a few minutes before, this would have merely seemed like common sense. But Jesus had changed everything.

James looked back to the sleeping Jesus. He looked almost the same as when the storm was raging. But which had *looked* more powerful then? What his eyes saw. But which really was more powerful? Jesus had killed the killer storm with a word.

James felt fear wash over him again. But it was a very different kind of fear. He thought, "Who then is this?" (v. 25).

As James looked back down at the water, the psalmist's words came to mind:

> For I know that the LORD is great,
>   and that our Lord is above all gods.
> Whatever the LORD pleases, he does,
>   in heaven and on earth,
>   in the seas and all deeps.
> He it is who makes the clouds rise at the end of the earth,
>   who makes lightnings for the rain
>   and brings forth the wind from his storehouses.
>   (Ps. 135:5–7)

James trembled.

○○

What Jesus did for James and the other disciples when he quieted the storm was a fear-transfer. One moment they feared the storm and the next moment they feared Jesus, with a holy, reverent fear. This storm was a gift from God to them because it taught them just how powerful Jesus was and deepened their faith in him. And it prepared them to weather other, even more deadly kinds of storms that lay ahead of them.

When the storms of life hit, they almost always appear stronger to us than God's Word. It is crucial for us to remember that our perceptions can be deceptive. When circumstances strike fear into our hearts, the question we must ask ourselves is, where is your faith?

What God wants is for you to trust what he says over what you see.

"Woman, where are they? Has no one condemned you?" She said, "No one, Lord." And Jesus said, "Neither do I condemn you; go, and from now on sin no more."

JOHN 8:10-11

2

"NEITHER DO I CONDEMN YOU"

THE ADULTERESS AND GUILT

John 8:2-11

"SHAME ON YOU, WHORE!"

She was married, but not to the man in whose arms she had been lying. Suddenly the door had burst open. Oh no! Instantly she was in the grasp of angry men who dragged her—and her forbidden secret—out into the street.

"Adulteress!" The name pierced her like an arrow. Loathing looks bored into her. Her life was undone in a moment, by her own doing.

And it was about to be crushed. They were talking about stoning! Oh my God, they're going to stone me! God, please have mercy!

But God's verdict on her case was clear:

> If a man is found lying with the wife of another man, both of them shall die, the man who lay with the woman, and the woman. So you shall purge the evil from Israel. (Deut. 22:22)

"Both shall die!" She was going to die! But where was he? Why hadn't they grabbed him?

No time to think. She was being half pushed, half pulled through Jerusalem. She was despised and rejected, as one from whom men hide their faces.

The temple? Why are we entering the temple? Suddenly she was thrust in front of a young man. A man behind her bawled, "Teacher, this woman has been caught in the act of adultery" (John 8:4). Oh God! Oh God! she begged silently. "Now in the Law Moses commanded us to stone such women. So what do you say?" (v. 5).

The teacher said nothing. He looked at her, then at her accusers. Then he bent down. She stood in frozen exposure. Why was he writing in the dirt? Men on either side of her were clenching brutal stones. Impatient prosecutors demanded a ruling.

The teacher stood back up. She held her breath, eyes on her feet. "Let him who is without sin among you be the first to throw a stone at her," he said (v. 7).

The crowd of judgment hushed to whispers. Confused, she risked a quick glance at him. He was writing in the dirt again. She heard murmurs and disgusted grunts around her. Then shuffling. A stone dropped with a dull thud beside her. Its former holder whispered, "Slut!" as he passed behind her. But they were leaving! No one grabbed her.

It took some courage to look around. Her accusers were gone. She looked back at the Teacher. He was standing, looking at her. She dropped her eyes again.

"Woman," he said, "where are they? Has no one condemned you?" She said, "No one, Lord." And Jesus said, "Neither do I condemn you; go, and from now on sin no more" (vv. 10–11).

○○

Forget for the moment the self-righteousness of the accusers and the apparent injustice of the adulterous man's absence. Did you really hear what Jesus said? "Neither do I condemn you." But this woman's guilt was *real*. She committed the crime of adultery. God, through Moses, commanded her death.

Now, if God the Son wouldn't condemn her, was God violating his own commandment and letting the guilty go unpunished? If so, then God was unjust. So how could Jesus possibly have said that to her?

Here's where the news gets really good. God fully intended for this sin of adultery to be punished to the full extent of his law. But she would not bear her punishment. She would go free. This young teacher, who would not condemn her, would be condemned in her place. Might he have written these words from Isaiah in the dirt?

> But he was pierced for our transgressions;
>   he was crushed for our iniquities;
> upon him was the chastisement that brought us peace,
>   and with his wounds we are healed.
> All we like sheep have gone astray;
>   we have turned—every one—to his own way;
> and the LORD has laid on him
> the iniquity of us all. (Isa. 53:5–6)

In a sense, every one of us is that woman. Our horrible sins—our shameful lusts, destructive tongues, murderous hatred, corrupting greed, covetous pride—stand exposed before God as starkly as in that temple courtyard. Our condemnation is deserved.

And yet, if you believe in Jesus, he speaks these stunning words to you: "Neither do I condemn you." Why? Because he has been condemned in your place. *All* your guilt has been removed. No stone of God's righteous wrath will crush you because Jesus was crushed for your iniquities.

Jesus was the only one in the crowd that day who could, in perfect righteousness, require the woman's death. And he was the only one who could, in perfect righteousness, pardon her. Mercy triumphed over judgment for her at great cost to Jesus. And the same is true for us.

So much glory is packed into the truth that "there is therefore now no condemnation for those who are in Christ Jesus" (Rom. 8:1).

"Go, and from now on sin no more."

JOHN 8:11

3

SHE STILL HAD TO GO HOME

THE ADULTERESS AND SIN'S CONSEQUENCES

Based on John 8:2–11

THE ADULTERESS WHO HAD been forgiven by Jesus in John 8 begins to head for home when she realizes what she still has to face: all the consequences of her sin.

◦ ◦

"Neither do I condemn you; go, and from now on sin no more" (v. 11).

These words were almost unbelievable. A half hour ago she had been dragged out of her illicit lover's house and shoved through the streets. Just minutes before, she had been bracing for the crushing stones of judgment.

Now those stones lay on the ground, the execution squad was gone, and the young rabbi with compassionate eyes was telling her she was free to go. Free? Where had her guilt gone? It was hard to comprehend. One moment she was a condemned sinner and the next she was condemnation free.

As she turned and began to walk toward home, she felt something strange. She was clean—cleaner than she could remember. How could that be? She hadn't done anything to deserve to be clean. There hadn't even been a ritual sacrifice or water cleansing according to the law yet. That rabbi had simply declared her guilt free, and it was so.

No one ever spoke like this man. She heard God when he spoke.

But after a few minutes of walking, it hit her: I have to go home. Fear shot through her. She wanted to bolt. The rabbi had forgiven her. But waiting at home was her betrayed husband. And her children. And her parents. And his parents. And her neighbors. And her illicit lover's family. She had brought shame and inexpressible pain upon them all. Her life was like a shattered pot, shards all over the floor, shattered by her sin. She almost longed to be buried by the stones.

But she still felt clean.

She drew her head-covering around her face and took a detour, walking streets where she might not be recognized. She needed time to think. And pray.

That was strange too. She hadn't prayed a heartfelt prayer in years. She hadn't wanted anything to do with God. She had merely been going through religious motions while secretly pursuing her own happiness in forbidden places. She had just tried to lay low and escape the Judge's attention.

But now all was different. As she thought of God, that fresh cleanness washed over her again, like it had when the rabbi spoke. She found herself wanting to run *to* God to hide rather than hide *from* him. Surprisingly, he was the one person she wanted to talk to most. This was new. God was no longer her condemning Judge. He had become a forgiving Father.

So she ducked into a lonely alley to repent of her horrible, selfish sin and to ask her Father for help with what seemed like an impossible situation. As she prayed, she heard the rabbi's words again, "Neither do I condemn you; go, and from now on sin no more." And then these words followed: "I am with you always (Matt. 28:20). With man it is impossible, but not with God. For all things are possible with God" (Mark 10:27).

With a new peace that surpassed her understanding, she caught her breath and headed for what was left of her home.

○○

We do not know what this woman faced after she left Jesus. But it must have been very painful.

Jesus removed the *guilt* of her sin, taking it and God's wrath against it upon himself. But he did not remove the *fact* that she had sinned and the relational pain that must have resulted. Maybe her husband was also saved and they were reconciled. Maybe he divorced her.

But whatever happened, she remained forgiven and clean. She was justified in God's eyes. In Jesus she became a new creature. Wearing Jesus's righteousness, the Father viewed her as if she had never sinned and as if she had perfectly obeyed, because Jesus became sin for her and he perfectly obeyed the Father on her behalf. And even the earthly consequences of her sin became a means of grace to her because God caused all of them to work together for her good.

And that's the hope we all need. We need the hope that we have been justified by the substitutionary atonement of Jesus. And we need the hope of the promise of Romans 8:28, that God will work all things, even the fallout from our past sins, together for good for us.

God's grace was sufficient for this woman, both to cover her sins and redeem her life. And, likewise, his grace will be sufficient for you.

And John, calling two of his disciples to him, sent them to the Lord, saying, "Are you the one who is to come, or shall we look for another?"

LUKE 7:18-19

4

DOUBT IN THE DARKNESS

JOHN THE BAPTIST AND DOUBT

Luke 7:18–28

AS JOHN THE BAPTIST sat in Herod Antipas's prison waiting likely execution, he was afflicted with doubts about Jesus.

○○

"Are you the one who is to come, or shall we look for another?" (v. 19).

This was a surprising question coming from John the Baptist.

It's unclear exactly when John first consciously knew that Jesus was the Son of God, whose way he had come to prepare. The apostle John quotes him, sometime after he baptized Jesus, as saying, "I myself did not know him" (John 1:31).

Now, this is remarkable because John's mother, Elizabeth, had known. She knew because John announced it to her *in utero* by leaping when she heard Mary's voice. Was she not allowed to tell him? We don't know. Regardless, John had known even before he knew.

What is clear is that when the revelation came, it was an overwhelming experience for John. That day, when Jesus approached him at the Jordan near Bethany, John couldn't contain the shout: "Behold, the Lamb of God, who takes away the sin of the world!" (John 1:29). With awe and trembling hands he had baptized his Lord. And then saw the Spirit descend and remain on him.

That day had also marked the beginning of the end of his ministry. From that point, he had joyfully directed people away from himself to follow Jesus. And they had.

Now he sat in Antipas's filthy prison. He had expected this. Prophets who rebuke sinful kings usually do not fare well. Unfortunately, he had not been an exception. Herodias wanted him dead. He was not optimistic that she would be denied her wish.

What he hadn't expected was to be tormented by such oppressive doubts and fears. Since the Jordan, John had not doubted that Jesus was the Christ. But stuck alone in this putrid cell he was assaulted by horrible, accusing thoughts.

What if he had been wrong? There had been many false prophets in Israel. What made him so sure that *he* wasn't one? What if he had led thousands astray?

There had also been many false messiahs. What if Jesus was another? So far, Jesus's ministry wasn't exactly what John had always imagined the Messiah's would look like. Could this imprisonment be God's judgment?

It felt as if God had left him and the Devil himself had taken his place. He tried to recall all the prophecies and signs that had seemed so clear to him before. But it was difficult to think straight. Comfort just wouldn't stick to his soul. Doubts buzzed around his brain like the flies around his face.

The thought of being executed for the sake of righteousness and justice he could bear. But he could not bear the thought that he might have been wrong about Jesus. His one task was to prepare the way of the Lord. If he had gotten that wrong, his ministry, his life, was in vain.

But even with his doubts, there remained in John a deep, unshakable trust in Jesus. Jesus would tell him the truth. He just needed to hear from him again.

So he sent two of his closest disciples to ask Jesus, "Are you the one who is to come, or shall we look for another?" (v. 20).

When the men relayed the question, the affection that radiated from Jesus was palpable. He loved John. And Jesus was familiar with John's sorrows and grief and the satanic storms that break on the saints when they are weak and alone. He too had been assaulted, and would be again.

So he invited John's faithful friends to sit near him as he healed many and delivered many from demonic prisons.

Then he turned to them with kind and moist eyes and said, "Tell John what you have seen and heard: the blind receive their sight, the lame walk, lepers are cleansed, and the deaf hear, the dead are raised up, the poor have good news preached to them" (v. 22). John would recognize Isaiah's prophecies in those words. This promise would bring the peace John needed to sustain him for the few difficult days he had remaining.

Out of love for his friend, Jesus didn't include Isaiah's phrase "proclaim liberty to the captives" (Isa. 61:1).

Then he added, "And blessed is the one who is not offended by me" (v. 23). Trust me, John.

When Jesus had sent John's disciples away, he said something stunning about John: no one born of women had ever been greater (v. 28). And the grace and patience of the Lord toward afflicted ones are more clearly seen in that he said this just after John had voiced his doubts.

○ ○

In this age, even the greatest, strongest saints experience deep darkness. None of us are spared sorrow or satanic oppression. Most of us suffer agonizing affliction at some point. Most of us will experience seasons when we feel as if we've been abandoned. Most of us will die hard deaths.

The Savior does not break the bruised reed. He hears our pleas for help and is patient with our doubts. He does not condemn us. He has paid completely for any sin that is exposed in our pain.

He does not always answer with the speed we desire, nor is his answer always the deliverance we hope for. But he will always send the help that is needed. His grace will always be sufficient for those who trust him. The hope we taste in the promises we trust will often be the sweetest thing we experience in this age. And the reward of God's fulfillment of these promises will be glorious beyond our imagination.

In John's darkness and pain, Jesus sent a promise to sustain John's faith. He will do the same for you.

And Zacchaeus stood and said to the Lord, "Behold, Lord, the half of my goods I give to the poor. And if I have defrauded anyone of anything, I restore it fourfold." And Jesus said to him, "Today salvation has come to this house, since he also is a son of Abraham. For the Son of Man came to seek and to save the lost."

LUKE 19:8-10

DISMEMBERING AN IDOL

ZACCHAEUS AND IDOLATRY

Based on Luke 19:1–10

ZACCHAEUS THE TAX COLLECTOR was converted, and he vowed to give back fourfold to anyone he had defrauded. Imagine a conversation that might have resulted when he returned the money.

○○

"Dad, there's a man at the door. He said his name is Zacchaeus."

"Zacchaeus!" Judah's face flushed with sudden anger. "What does *he* want?" Under his breath he muttered, "The little vermin." His young daughter didn't need to hear that.

"I don't know."

Judah moved brusquely past his daughter, clenching his jaw. If the little weasel even hints at more money, I swear . . . a thunderstorm of violent thoughts broke in his mind.

When he saw Zacchaeus, he exploded, "WHAT?" Zacchaeus reeled slightly from the verbal blow.

"I'm here to return something to you, Judah."

"What do you mean?" The tone sounded more like, "Get out of my sight!"

Zacchaeus held out a small moneybag. Judah was suspiciously confused. This man had robbed half of Jericho collecting taxes for Tiberius. No one was more conniving and slippery with words. Fearing some kind of setup, Judah didn't move.

"What are you doing, Zacchaeus?" Cynicism hissed through Judah's teeth.

"I'm dismembering my idol."

Judah's fiery glare turned to stony bewilderment. "What are you talking about?"

"Judah, I know how strange this must sound. And you have every reason not to trust me. I'm here because I've defrauded you. I've charged you more taxes than Rome required and kept them for my wicked little self. I know that you and everyone else knows that. But now I've come to ask your forgiveness for sinning against you like that, and to make restitution. That's what's in this bag."

Zacchaeus held it out again. This time Judah tentatively took it. He looked inside. "There's a lot in here. It's got to be more than you overcharged me."

"Yes. It's four times what I overcharged you. I've got all the records, you know." Zacchaeus smiled.

"Why are you giving me four times what you owe me?" Judah's distrust was not dispelled.

"I'm keeping a vow. I promised Jesus that I would repay everyone I defrauded fourfold."

"You mean the Rabbi Jesus? You know him?"

"I do now. He's in town, as you know. And the other day I wanted to get a glimpse of him. But being, uh, short-legged, I figured the only way I'd see him was from a tree! Wouldn't you know, as Jesus passes by he stops, looks up at silly me in the sycamore and says, 'Zacchaeus, hurry and come down, for I must stay at your house today.'"

Judah gave him a puzzled look.

Zacchaeus said, "I know, I know! I was as shocked as anyone! How did he know my name, right? So Jesus and his disciples come to my house and in a matter of minutes my world falls apart and comes together."

"Falls apart and comes together?"

"Judah, when I was a boy, I was in awe of what I thought money did for people. It seemed to open all the doors to power and pleasure. So I vowed to myself that whatever it took, I was going to be rich. And I kept that vow. Back then I had no idea how empty being rich would be. But, up till two days ago, I figured it was still better than the alternative.

"But as I sat in my home with Jesus and his disciples, who have *nothing*—nothing but *God*—Judah, I've never seen happier people in my life! And as Jesus spoke, it was like his words were alive. My heart burned with a longing for God I had never felt before! And with a deep shame that I traded him for *money*.

"Then it hit me like a cedar beam: *I'm poor, not rich!* They had God; I had a dead idol: money. They were rich; I was no more than a beggar. They were free. But the only doors money ever opened for me led to lonely dungeons. My world, as I had known it, fell apart.

"And there sat Jesus, looking at me as if he could read me like a scroll. Everything in me just wanted to follow him. I wanted the forgiveness and salvation he's been preaching about. For the first time in my life I wanted God more than . . . *anything!* Suddenly, it was like life never made more sense. Before I knew it, I was on my feet vowing in front of everyone that, well, that I would dismember my idol."

"Give away your money."

"Right. Well, some of it is *your* money."

This time Judah smiled.

Later, Judah's wife found him staring at a small moneybag on the table.

"What's that?"

"A tax refund."

"A what?"

"I think we need to go hear Rabbi Jesus."

"Rabbi Jesus? Why?"

"I think we're poor."

○ ○

Some of our idols need to be dismembered for us to be free of them. Jesus knows what they are and how to help us see them. It may feel like we are losing our world to lose them.

That's okay. Jesus said, "For whoever would save his life will lose it, but whoever loses his life for my sake will find it. For what will it profit a man if he gains the whole world and forfeits his soul?" (Matt. 16:25–26). And as Jim Elliot said, "He is no fool who gives what he cannot keep to gain that which he cannot lose."[1] There are losses that turn out to be great gain.

"Take care, and be on your guard against all covetousness, for one's life does not consist in the abundance of his possessions" (Luke 12:15).

---

[1] Jim Elliot in Elisabeth Elliot, *In the Shadow of the Almighty* (New York: Harper and Row, 1958), 108. See http://www2.wheaton.edu/bgc/archives/faq/20.htm/.

And they put forward two, Joseph called Barsabbas, who was also called Justus, and Matthias. And they prayed and said, "You, Lord, who know the hearts of all, show which one of these two you have chosen to take the place in this ministry and apostleship from which Judas turned aside to go to his own place." And they cast lots for them, and the lot fell on Matthias, and he was numbered with the eleven apostles.

ACTS 1:23-26

6

WHY ARE YOU DISAPPOINTED?

JOSEPH BARSABBAS AND DISAPPOINTMENT

Acts 1:15–26

JOSEPH BARSABBAS WAS A candidate to replace Judas Iscariot as one of the Twelve. But when the lot was cast it "fell on Matthias" (Acts 1:26). Joseph was dis-appointed (not appointed). That must have been disappointing.

The Bible never mentions Joseph again. But tradition says he later became Bishop of Eleutheropolis (about thirty miles southwest of Jerusalem) and died a faithful martyr. Imagine what Joseph's disappointment taught him about trusting God, and how years later he might have counseled a disappointed young disciple.

○ ○

Bishop Joseph looked at his sullen disciple. "You're disappointed."

"Yes," replied Primus.

"Why?"

The answer seemed obvious. Primus suspected a teaching moment. "I was just hoping for the appointment to the Antioch church that Asher received."

"That's the *event* of your disappointment. My question is *why* are you disappointed?"

Suspicion confirmed. Primus just wanted to sulk in peace. Maybe if he downplayed his disgruntlement the lesson would be shorter. "Asher's a good friend. I'm glad for him. I just thought studying at Antioch would be a great opportunity. I'll get over it."

The sage shepherd was not easily dodged. "Studying at Antioch *is* a great opportunity. You were not wrong to desire it. My question remains: *why* are you disappointed?" Primus's face flushed with impatience. "Well, if Antioch is a great opportunity and I'm missing the opportunity, isn't it okay to be disappointed?"

"That depends. What kind of disappointment are we talking about?" asked the Bishop.

"I don't understand what you mean."

"The *event* of disappointment is when we are removed from or, as in your case, we are not granted an appointment—a role or responsibility or opportunity of some kind. These events can happen for reasons both good and evil. The *emotion* of disappointment, which is what we're talking about, results when that event occurs contrary to our hopes. Whether or not it's okay to feel disappointed depends on which soil it's growing in."

Primus looked at him blankly.

"Disappointment is similar to anger in that there are legitimate and illegitimate reasons to feel it. If some evil has caused the event of our disappointment, the emotion could be right because evil defiles God's glory. But whatever the cause, if our emotion is growing in the soil of love and faith, it will produce a righteous fruit, like contentment or just action or gracious forbearance. But if its roots are in the soil of selfishness, it will bear unrighteous fruit, like jealousy and selfish ambition, which are themselves evil and defile God's glory."

The young man looked out the window.

"Primus, what is my favorite quote from the greatest man born of women?"

"'A person cannot receive even one thing unless it is given him from heaven'" (John 3:27).

"Right. So, do you believe that?"

"Yes. I know that God ultimately decrees these things." Looking back to the Bishop, Primus said, "But let me ask you a question. When the lot fell to Matthias, didn't you feel disappointed?

"Yes, I did. I felt quite disappointed—and a bit embarrassed."

"Was that wrong? I mean you were almost one of the Twelve. It just seems natural to feel disappointed over something like that, even if it was God's will."

"Well, aspiring to apostleship wasn't wrong. But when the Lord appointed another, and *dis*appointed me, I found that much of my disappointment was rooted in a frustrated desire for my own glory. And that was wrong. I was doubting the promise that "no good thing does he withhold from those who walk uprightly" (Ps. 84:11). I was doubting that the One who was crucified for my sin and called me out of darkness into his marvelous light (1 Pet. 2:9) really had my best in mind. And it exposed my selfish ambition. It wasn't until the lot fell on Matthias that I realized how much my love of reputation affected my desire for the position."

Primus stared thoughtfully at the floor.

"The emotion of disappointment is never neutral, Primus. It is not vague and detached. It has roots directly connected to something we believe. Jesus wants you follow the roots. If you find that sin is feeding your emotion of disappointment, then your event of disappointment is a kindness meant to lead you to repentance.

"And, like me, one day you may look back on your disappointment as the best thing that never happened to you."

○○

A very precious promise from Jesus to remember is this: "You did not choose me but I chose you and appointed you that you should go and bear fruit" (John 15:16).

But if Jesus appoints us, it also implies that he will disappoint us—meaning, there are some appointments from which Jesus will remove us, and others that he will not grant to us.

At these times we must "trust in the LORD with all [our] heart, and . . . not lean on [our] own understanding" (Prov. 3:5). We seldom understand all of his purposes. When disappointment comes through an evil earthly cause, we need to call to mind the truth that Joseph discovered after being disappointed by his brothers: "You meant evil against me, but God meant it for good" (Gen. 50:20). And in all cases, remember that in Christ, God is pursuing us *only* with goodness and mercy (Ps. 23:6). His promise is this: "He who did not spare his own Son but gave him up for us all, how will he not also with him graciously give us all things?" (Rom. 8:32).

Follow your emotion of disappointment to its roots. If you find unbelief and pride giving it life, apply the herbicide of God's promises for you.

As they were going along the road, someone said to him, "I will follow you wherever you go."

LUKE 9:57

7

CAN YOU BEAR UNCERTAINTY?

WOULD-BE DISCIPLE AND PROVISION

Luke 9:57

UNCERTAINTY IS A DIFFICULT thing to bear. We want to know where the provision is going to come from or if we're going to die of this disease or how this child is going to turn out or if our job will still be there next month.

But Jesus makes it clear that his disciples must be able to bear uncertainty if they are to follow him.

○○

"I will follow you wherever you go."

I'm sure that whoever made this public declaration to Jesus was sincere. He likely had heard him preach and seen him perform amazing signs and wonders. As Jesus's fame increased, so did the number of his would-be disciples.

What the person might not have known was that at that moment Jesus was homeless.

Jesus and his cohort were traveling south from Galilee. He had set his face to go to Jerusalem, where his resolute purpose was to die. But to get there he had to cross through Samaria.

At the time there was a lot of bad blood between Jews and Samaritans. More precisely, to the Jews it was the Samaritans who had the bad blood. They were the result of centuries of intermarriage and religious syncretism between Jews and Israel's former Gentile conquerors.

Over many years the Samaritans had developed their own version of the Scriptures and built their own temple on their own mountain. Their beliefs were profane distortions of Jewish orthodoxy. Therefore, the Jews had "no dealings with Samaritans" (John 4:9) and vice versa.

But Jesus had made a bit of a name for himself among the Samaritans because he had dealings with them. For a Jew, Jesus spoke with and about Samaritans with unprecedented kindness and compassion. In fact, near the town of Sychar he had spoken with a woman of questionable reputation, and as a result she and many other Samaritans believed that Jesus really was the Messiah.[1]

But to the Samaritans in the town where Jesus wanted to spend the night, that didn't matter. What mattered was that his face was set toward Jerusalem. And if that was the case, they wanted no dealings with him (Luke 9:52–53). Jesus experienced discrimination.

This made Jesus's disciples indignant. The Samaritans weren't just heretics, they were ingrates. James and John wanted to burn the town off the map (Luke 9:54).

But Jesus hadn't come to judge the world. He had come to save it (John 12:47). So he simply moved on without any place to stay the night.

So when an adoring fan publicly announced his desire to follow him anywhere, Jesus deglamorized things a bit by replying, "Foxes have holes, and the birds of the air have nests, but the Son of Man has nowhere to lay his head" (Luke 9:58).

○ ○

God doesn't tell us how that would-be disciple responded

---

[1] See John 4:1–42.

because what's important is the implied question: can you bear uncertainty? Can you bear not knowing how God is going to provide for your most urgent needs and still trust that he will?

Jesus gave that man, and us, fair warning. To follow him is to follow a homeless man and become "strangers and exiles on the earth" (Heb. 11:13). There are simply going to be times when obedience or faithfulness to his call means we aren't sure where the provision for our needs will come from. Unforeseen circumstances will occur. Plans will fall through. The salary might not allow for much retirement savings. Financial support might need to be raised. A thief may break in and steal. Economies may collapse. Radical generosity may be required to meet another's desperate need. A debilitating illness may befall. Religious or racial discrimination may deny.

When these things happen, we are often tempted to fear because our earthly security is being removed. But we should not be surprised. "A servant is not greater than his master" (John 13:16). If these things happened to Jesus, they will also happen to us.

Jesus does not want us to be governed by fear at such times. He wants us governed by faith. The uncertainty we are faced with is only *apparent* uncertainty. Our future and our provision and our ultimate triumph are certain to God. He has all the foreknowledge, power, and resources necessary to insure these, and he has the desire to turn everything for good for those who love him and are called by him (Rom. 8:28).

Apparently uncertain seasons are often some of the most powerful moments we experience with God in this age. More than seasons of security and prosperity, they demonstrate that God exists and rewards those who seek him (Heb. 11:6).

So if you are in one of those seasons, take heart. God is graciously allowing you to experience the reality that he "acts for those who wait for him" (Isa. 64:4).

"Unless I see in his hands the mark of the nails, and place my finger into the mark of the nails, and place my hand into his side, I will never believe." . . . "My Lord and my God!"

JOHN 20:25, 28

8

"I WILL NEVER BELIEVE"

THOMAS AND SKEPTICISM

John 20:24–29

BELIEVING WHAT WE CANNOT see is hard. All of us are skeptics to some degree, some more than others. But there is often more going on inside a skeptic than meets the eye. And, as we see in Thomas's experience, Jesus knows how to reach them.[1]

○○

Jesus's death had been difficult and confusing for everyone. Having been welcomed into Jerusalem like a king, he was dead before the week was over. And when the shepherd was struck, the sheep scattered (Mark 14:27). But they regathered in a secret hideout in Jerusalem.

On Sunday things took a weird twist. It began with Mary Magdalene insisting that she had seen Jesus alive that morning. True, Jesus's body disappearing was admittedly strange. But still, everyone knew Jesus had really died. No one could really believe Mary's claim, except maybe John.

Then later in the day Peter announced that he also had seen Jesus alive. This troubled Thomas. But he figured he

---

[1] Thomas's skepticism over Jesus's resurrection is recorded in this text, but the chronology of events are drawn from a combination of all the Gospels' accounts of the days following the crucifixion.

could cut Peter some slack. After denying Jesus publicly, who could blame Peter for desperately wishing it to be true? He just needed time.

But then Cleopas burst into the house Sunday night claiming that he had walked—*walked!*—with Jesus to Emmaus that afternoon. What Thomas found particularly hard to believe was that Cleopas and his friend hadn't recognized Jesus the entire time until dinner, when *poof!* he just disappeared.

Well, this excited everyone else, but Thomas only felt agitated. He desperately missed Jesus too, but he wasn't going to let grief make him believe bizarre things. Jesus was dead.

Yet he didn't feel like dousing everyone's unreal hope with a wet blanket of reality. They weren't ready to hear it anyway. Thomas decided he needed to clear his head with a walk. By himself.

So after whispering a discreet excuse to Nathanael, he managed to slip outside without notice. After being very careful not to betray the hideout, he covered his head and started down an empty street.

The quiet was refreshing. But the walk wasn't as helpful as he had hoped. The Jesus sightings disturbed him, especially because the witnesses were credible. He knew them. They certainly weren't liars. They weren't unstable. None were given to delusions. Peter, particularly, was a rock of reason.

Then a rush of memories from the past three years flowed through Thomas's mind. He had seen so many things that would have been unbelievable if he hadn't *seen* them. Most haunting right now was Lazarus.

And Jesus *had* seemed to know that he was going to die in Jerusalem. He had said those strange things about death and resurrection.

Suddenly Thomas realized he was arguing with *himself.* His agitation really wasn't over his friends' failure to face the facts.

The facts, in fact, were now confusing. He was agitated because part of him actually believed Jesus was alive again. That's what Jesus had meant, wasn't it? But this frustrated the skeptic in him who took pride in being a man of common sense. A resurrection just seemed too incredible to be true.

The more he thought, the less sure he became. No one knew where Jesus's body was. Those who claimed to have seen him were people he trusted. It would make sense of certain prophecies. Could it be?

Show me the body! his skeptic side shouted. At least Lazarus could be seen and touched in Bethany by any doubter. So if Jesus really was alive, why this "hide and seek" game? Wouldn't he just show himself to them all?

He'd believe Jesus was alive when he *saw* him alive.

When Thomas returned to the house, four of his friends pounced on him, "We have seen the Lord (v. 24), Thomas! It's all true! He was just with us! Where were you?"

Thomas felt a surge of shocked unbelief. Then he felt regret for having left. Then he felt isolated. He was now the only one who hadn't seen Jesus.

In self-pity–fueled anger, he blurted out with more conviction than he felt, "Unless I see in his hands the mark of the nails, and place my finger into the mark of the nails, and place my hand into his side, I will never believe" (v. 25).

Most of his friends were dismayed. But Peter just watched him, smiling slightly.

The following eight days were long and lonely for Thomas. His friends were gracious. No one debated him. It was, in fact, their calm confidence in Jesus's resurrection that aggravated Thomas's growing conviction that he was wrong. Outside he tried to maintain a façade of resolute intellectual skepticism, but inside he was wrestling and melting and wanting more than anything to see Jesus too.

And then it happened. Thomas was staring at the floor, sinking again under the fear that maybe Jesus had rejected him because of his stubborn unbelief. If so, he knew he deserved it. Then someone gasped. He looked up, and his heart leaped into his throat! Jesus was standing across the room looking at him. "Peace be with you" (v. 26).

Thomas could hardly breathe. Jesus spoke to him, "Put your finger here, and see my hands; and put out your hand, and place it in my side. Do not disbelieve, but believe" (v. 27).

All objections and resistance in Thomas evaporated. And in tears of repentance, relief, and worship Thomas dropped on his knees before Jesus and exclaimed, "My Lord and my God!" (v. 28).

○○

Be patient and gracious with the skeptics in your life. Don't assume their outward confidence accurately reflects their inward condition. Keep praying for them and share what seems helpful when it seems helpful. Keep confidently and humbly following Jesus. And trust his timing. He knows best how and when to reveal himself to them.

About that time Herod the king laid violent hands on some who belonged to the church. He killed James the brother of John with the sword.

ACTS 12:1-2

9

THE NIGHT THE ANGEL DIDN'T COME

JAMES ZEBEDEE AND DEATH

Acts 12:1–2

LUKE SAYS IT SO briefly and matter-of-fact: Herod "killed James the brother of John with the sword."

In the flow of the story, this little phrase sets the stage for Peter's dramatic prison rescue by the angel. So that's what we remember. When Peter later wrote, "The Lord knows how to rescue the godly from trials" (2 Pet. 2:9), this is the sort of rescue that easily comes to mind.

But the night that James sat in prison, the angel didn't come.

I'm sure he prayed for an angel. He knew God could send one if he wanted to. An angel had already rescued him and the other disciples once before (Acts 5:17–21).

But this night there was no bright light, no chains falling off, no sleeping guards. Just desperate prayers and fitful dozing—if he slept at all.

In the morning, James was still in jail when the dreaded voice of the captain of the guard shouted, "Bring out the prisoner!" There was an anxiety-filled, prayerful walk to the place of execution. There was a pronouncement of guilt. Possibly there was an offer of pardon in exchange for recanting, followed by a refusal. There was a raised sword. No angel voice to stop the hand like Abraham on the mountain (Gen. 22:11–12).

There was a wince of fearful anticipation. The sword came down. No deliverance.

Or was there?

God allowed the sword to fall on James just as intentionally as he opened Peter's prison door. So the death of James is as crucial for us to remember as the rescue of Peter.

Why did God let James die?

This question is relevant because at some point most of us will find ourselves facing death, pleading for deliverance, and not receiving what we think we are asking for. And it points to a difficult lesson that all of Jesus's disciples must learn: Jesus often has different priorities than we do. What may feel desperately urgent to us may not be urgent to him—at least not in the same way.

Remember how Jesus slept in the boat during the storm? The disciples panicked at the fear of drowning and cried out, "Teacher, do you not care that we are perishing?" (Mark 4:38). He calmed the storm and then said to them, "Why are you so afraid? Have you still no faith?" (v. 40). Jesus's lesson was clear: you're afraid of the wrong thing. Don't fear what or who can kill your body, but fear and trust me because I rule over storms and death (Matt. 10:28). Jesus knew that there were more dangerous storms ahead for the disciples, ones that really would kill them. They needed to know whom to fear.

And so do we. Unless Jesus returns first, every one of us will face a storm that will kill us. And our initial response may be similar to the disciples' in the boat: Jesus, don't you care that I am perishing? In that moment we must remember that he cares deeply. He who wept beside Lazarus's tomb will weep with us—and he will raise us. And we must remember that he knows what death is like and will be with us through it and help us say as he said to the Father, "Not as I will, but as you will" (Matt. 26:39).

And we also need to remember James, who faced death "refusing to accept release that [he] might rise again to a better life" (Heb. 11:35). There is the real key to understanding Acts 12:2: Jesus let James die because he had a better life to give him.

James was not being neglected by Jesus. He was in fact the first of the Twelve to experience what Jesus prayed for in John 17:24: "Father, I desire that they also, whom you have given me, may be with me where I am, to see my glory that you have given me because you loved me before the foundation of the world." Peter's deliverance from prison was remarkable. But he lived to die another day. James experienced the true deliverance: death being swallowed up (1 Cor. 15:54) by the Resurrection and the Life (John 11:25).

And that is what Jesus longs and intends to give to us too. That's what he endured the Father's wrath on the cross to purchase for us. He wants us to see and enjoy and rejoice in his glory forever.

There will come a time when Jesus's prayer for us to be with him will overrule our prayer for prolonged earthly life. And when it does, we will experience a life so far better, richer, fuller, purer, and more joyful that we will shake our heads in wonder that we ever pleaded to stay.

May God increase our "desire . . . to depart and be with Christ, for that is far better" (Phil. 1:23).

And her husband Joseph, being a just man and unwilling to put her to shame, resolved to divorce her quietly.

MATTHEW 1:19

10

FACING A PAINFUL DECISION

JOSEPH THE CARPENTER AND GUIDANCE

Matthew 1:18–25

HAVE YOU EVER WONDERED why God sent the angel to inform Mary that she would conceive the Messiah by the Holy Spirit, yet forced Joseph to agonize over what to do about Mary's pregnancy before sending the angel to him? Imagine what those throbbing, awkward hours must have been like for him.

○ ○

Joseph felt a twinge of anxiety. He sensed something unusual in Mary's request that he come as soon as possible.

When he arrived, she was standing under the tree near her father's house where, as a betrothed couple, they were given some supervised privacy. Mary wasn't herself. She was staring at the ground. She seemed burdened.

"Mary, is something wrong?"

She looked up at him intensely. "Joseph . . ." She paused. "I'm pregnant."

A blast of shock and disbelief stunned him, blowing away all his coherent thoughts for a moment. His legs quavered. He grabbed at the tree to steady himself. It felt solid, rooted.

He stared at her. He was numb. No words came. Everything seemed surreal.

Mary was still looking at him with her intense eyes. He saw no shame in them. No defensiveness, no defiance. Not even tears. They looked . . . innocent. And they were searching his eyes for an answer.

Mary broke the charged silence. "What I need to tell you next I don't even know how to say."

Joseph leaned harder into the tree, bracing himself. He looked down to Mary's feet. Her feet. They looked just the same as they did when he believed she was pure.

That was what made everything so strange. Mary looked as chaste as she ever did. If she had been the flirtatious type or even had some discernible character weakness, this news might have been comprehendible. But Mary was literally the very last person he would have suspected of unfaithfulness. He could not imagine her with another lover. He didn't want to know who it was.

"I know this will be very difficult to believe. But I need you to listen to me." Still looking at Mary's feet, Joseph's nod was barely detectable.

"I have not been unfaithful to you."

Joseph raised his eyes to hers. Rape? That might explain her innocence. But why wouldn't she have told me—

"God has caused me to become pregnant."

This statement fluttered around his mind, looking for a place to land. It found none.

"Joseph, I know how it sounds. But I'm telling you the truth." Then Mary described an angelic visit and the message she had received. She was to bear a son, conceived by the Holy Spirit, who would be called the Son of the Most High who would sit on David's throne forever. God was the baby's father. Mary was pregnant with the Messiah.

She sounded as sane as ever. Nothing about her was different. Except that she was claiming to be pregnant with God's child. He felt like his brain was exploding. Was she adding blasphemy to adultery? He could not conceive of her being capable of either.

The silence was long, straining at the seams with tension.

"I . . . I don't even know what to say to you, Mary. I can't even think straight. I need to be alone."

Joseph spent the late afternoon walking up on the brow of the hill that overlooked Nazareth. Things were clear up there. From this height he could see the Sea of Galilee to the east, and to the west he could just see the blue Mediterranean on the horizon.

But he could not see how Mary's story could be true. There was nothing like it in the Torah or the Prophets that he could remember. "God, show me what to do!" He must have prayed this a hundred times.

The sun was setting as Joseph reached the nearly finished house that was to be their home. Just that morning, working on the roof, he had been dreaming of the happy voices of children—his and Mary's children—that would someday fill this house. That dream was now dead. His decision was made. Mary's claims were too incredible, maybe even delusional. He needed to end the betrothal. But he resolved to do it as quietly as possible to shield Mary from avoidable shame. He still loved her.

That night he fell asleep, exhausted from grief. And then the angel came to him and resurrected his dream with a wildness and wonder that was beyond comprehension.

○ ○

God chose Joseph for his role just as he chose Mary for hers. But he dealt with them differently. He could have told them both in advance about Jesus, but he didn't. He informed

Mary but not Joseph. Then God allowed what must have been a horribly awkward conversation to happen.

At that point, Joseph faced a very painful decision. And God did not rescue him from it immediately. He allowed Joseph to struggle in grief and bewilderment for a time. Being a just man (Matt. 1:19), Joseph assessed Mary's claims in the integrity of his heart, and, I think we can assume, with a deep trust in God. He made the best decision that he could, one he believed was both just and merciful.

But it turned out to be the wrong one, because God was doing far more abundantly than Joseph could ask or think (Eph. 3:20). And that's when God, full of mercy, intervened. He gently corrected Joseph and gave him the guidance he needed.

God will not spare us from all awkward and painful decisions. Neither will he spare us from all wrong decisions resulting from our fallen finiteness, even if they are made in the integrity of our hearts. God has his purposes in all of these. But what we can trust him to do is faithfully give us the correction and guidance we need at the time he deems right.

And she gave birth to her firstborn son and wrapped him in swaddling cloths and laid him in a manger, because there was no place for them in the inn.

LUKE 2:7

11

STABLES OF DESPERATION ARE THE BIRTHPLACES OF GOD'S GRACE

JOSEPH THE CARPENTER AND TRUST

Luke 2:1–7

THE FIRST CHRISTMAS NIGHT was a holy night. But it was not a silent night. *All* was not calm. After walking a hundred miles, Joseph arrived in an overcrowded Bethlehem, with a wife in advanced labor, only to find that "there was no place for them in the inn."

○ ○

"We are completely full. We can't take another person."

"Please, my wife is about to give birth! We'll take anything with a little privacy."

Compassion and exasperation mixed in the fatigued inn-keeper's eyes. His tired hand rubbed over his head. "Look, I would give you our own quarters, but we've already given them to others. People are in every nook and cranny. There is no room, especially to have a baby."

Back in Nazareth, Joseph had felt so confident. He knew nothing about assisting in births. That was women's domain.

But God had sent his angel to Mary and to him. God had caused Mary to get pregnant. God had turned the stream of mighty Augustus's heart (Prov. 21:1) so that the Messianic prophesy about Bethlehem would be fulfilled. Surely God would provide their needs when they arrived. After all, this Child was God's Son!

But now Joseph was growing desperate. Bethlehem was overrun with people. The Roman census got the Messiah to Bethlehem, but it left him no place to lay his head.

"Are there other inns here?"

"No. Bethlehem can't keep two inns in business—usually. You don't have any family close by?"

Mary cried out in pain.

Nearly frantic, Joseph spared his words. "No. Please! Is there anyone who could take us in?"

"Everyone I know is already housing guests."

Please, God! Please! We need a place! Give us a room! Send your angel! Do something!

The two men looked vacantly at each other for a tense five seconds. Then Joseph choked out, "Please, we'll take *anything!*

At that moment a woman appeared behind the innkeeper and said, "We have a stable in the back."

"Rachel,[1] his wife is about to give birth! We can't put her in the stable!"

"I heard," she answered. "But leaving her in the street would be worse, Jacob. I'll get some blankets and clean straw." She looked at Joseph, "I'll meet you in the back. I can help with the birth too." She began to move then stopped. "What's your wife's name?"

"Mary."

"Tell Mary it will be okay. God will help you."

---

[1] "Rachel" and "Jacob" are fictitious names. I am using the same names for these characters and coordinating events in harmony with John Piper's moving book, *The Innkeeper* (Wheaton, IL: Crossway, 1998).

"Thank you!" Joseph said. *Thank you, God!*

But relief collided with regret inside of him. Rachel's help was a gift. But the stable? That's the best he could provide for his trusting wife and this holy Child? How could God's Son be born in a stable?

Mary cried out again, "Joseph!"

No more time. With gentle swiftness Joseph picked Mary up and carried her toward the back of the inn.

Mary's breathing was labored. "They have a room?"

Joseph felt a stab of shame. "The only thing left is the stable. It'll be okay. We'll make it clean. The innkeeper's wife is going to help us. God is providing."

"Thank you, God!" she whispered. And then squeezed Joseph's neck as another pain seized her and pushed the Light further into the world.

○ ○

A stable was not where Joseph wanted to be that night. It held no romance for him. He was only there out of desperation.

But the stable was not about Joseph or Mary. It was about the Son of God making himself nothing (Phil. 2:7). He had come to humble himself to unfathomable depths. So he borrowed a stable for his birth. Later, after an excruciating death to make propitiation for our sins (1 John 4:10), he would borrow a tomb (Matt. 27:59–60).

But Joseph likely didn't grasp any of that in Bethlehem. In the mayhem of the moment, all he knew was that the best he could do for Mary and the Messiah was a stable full of real and ritual uncleanness. And to battle fear and shame, all he could have done was trust that somehow God, who could have provided differently, had some mysterious purpose in this humiliation.

And in that is a Christmas word to us. There are times, while seeking to follow God faithfully, we find ourselves in a desperate moment, forced to a place we would not choose to go. It's then we must remember: our lives and circumstances are not ultimately about us (1 Cor. 6:19–20). They are about Jesus Christ.

The Father has purposes for us and our hardships that extend far beyond us. What often appear like misfortunes in the moment later prove to be means of great mercies.

In your place of desperation it may be that what you need most is not less turmoil, but more trust. For God chooses stables of desperation as the birthplaces of his overwhelming grace.

Behold, an angel of the Lord appeared to Joseph in a dream.

MATTHEW 2:13

12

(UN)PLANNED DETOURS

JOSEPH THE CARPENTER AND GUIDANCE

Matthew 1–2

"THE HEART OF MAN plans his way, but the LORD establishes his steps" (Prov. 16:9). As Jesus's earthly father discovered, this is just another way of saying that when your plans are detoured and redirected, you find out who's really charting the course.

○ ○

Nazareth. It felt good to Joseph to be back home. The same old market and the same old merchants. The same old neighbors with the same old complaints. The same old synagogue and the same old rabbi.

Oddly, though, the normalcy felt a bit strange after the unexpected adventures of the past couple of years. What an odyssey this simple Galilean carpenter had been on.

It had all started with Mary's world-shaking pregnancy announcement that took an angel to help him believe. He had hardly stopped reeling from that news when he was hit with the census decree from Rome.

Joseph recalled the anger he had felt. A vain emperor a world away was ordering people to their ancestral cities to register. God forbid that Augustus lose any possible tax revenue from peasants. For Joseph, as a descendent of King David, this meant a royal one-hundred-mile walk to Bethlehem. It seemed outrageously unjust. Not only would this disrupt his business and incur travel expenses he could not afford, but Mary would be in advanced pregnancy!

He remembered venting his exasperation to a friend who had replied, "May God send Messiah soon and deliver us from these tyrants!" And then to cheer Joseph had added, "Hey, maybe you'll see the Messiah there! You know what the prophet said,

> But you, O Bethlehem Ephrathah,
>   who are too little to be among the clans of Judah,
> from you shall come forth for me
>   one who is to be ruler in Israel,
> whose coming forth is from of old,
>   from ancient days. (Mic. 5:2)

His friend might as well have hit Joseph on the head with a beam. All at once he saw it! Augustus in all his imperial pomp was merely a tool in the hand of God to fulfill Scripture. His anger melted into awe-filled joy. Yes, Joseph most certainly would see the Messiah in Bethlehem.

In fact, after Jesus's incredible birth, Joseph had fully expected to make Bethlehem their new permanent home. Surely that's what the prophet Micah meant. And he had just started to get his business going when the angel of his dreams came again, shortly after the surprise visit by the Persian magi. "Flee to Egypt and remain there until I tell you." Herod wanted to murder their baby!

Joseph had felt anger rise against Herod. And a wave of fear. The Egyptian border was another one-hundred-mile foot journey for his wife and child, mostly through desert.

But he quickly remembered. If Augustus was God's tool, what was Herod? God had his reasons to send his Son to

Egypt. So Joseph snuck his family out of town in the cover of night.

Egypt. That was one place Joseph had never expected to see, much less live in. He hadn't had any idea how he would feed and house his family there. But he need not have worried. God provided for them like he had all along.

And then after a few months another dream and another commission: Herod had died, and Joseph was to take the child back to Israel. Joseph assumed this meant returning to Bethlehem.

But he soon learned that Herod's son, Archelaus, was ruling over Judea. Archelaus was a cruel chip off the brutal block. If he got wind of a Messiah in Bethlehem, no doubt another assassination would be attempted. One more angelic dream visit, and it was back to Nazareth.

And who knew how long that would last . . .

○ ○

One thing Joseph learned very quickly after God had drafted him to be the earthly father of Jesus was that his own plans were not a thing to be grasped. Whatever future he had originally imagined for himself and Mary evaporated in the heat of a reality determined by Another.

And as he followed the path of faith, he repeatedly found it taking unpredictable turns: a Roman census, a grueling trip during the hardest part of pregnancy, a birth in a barn, no steady income, an assassination attempt, two desert crossings on foot with an infant, living in a foreign country, and waiting on God for last-minute guidance and provision. This path was difficult, dangerous, expensive, time-consuming, and career delaying.

And it was all God's will.

Like Joseph's, the unplanned, inefficient detours of our lives are planned by God. God's ways are not our ways (Isa. 55:8–9). They are frequently bewildering to us, but they are always better because God is orchestrating far more than we see or know in every unexpected event and delay.

So when you find yourself suddenly moving in a direction you had not planned, take heart; the Great Planner has something much better in mind for you and countless others.

Do not be afraid and do not be dismayed at this great horde, for the battle is not yours but God's.

2 CHRONICLES 20:15

13

"DO NOT BE AFRAID"

JEHOSHAPHAT AND FEAR

2 Chronicles 20:1–30

THE ARMIES OF MOAB, Ammon, and Edom were on the move. Destination: Jerusalem. These were relatives of Israel, Moab and Ammon being descendants of Lot and Edom of Esau. But this was no family reunion. This was a slaughter in the making.

These three nations bordered Israel and Judah on the east and south. And since the reigns of David and Solomon, they had off-and-on been subject to the kings of Israel, paying a tribute tax and providing forced labor.

But it had been over sixty years since Solomon's death, and Israel had split into two kingdoms. Its strength was divided. And the northern kingdom was weakened from its battles with Syria. The time was ripe. If they joined forces now, these kin could crush the army of Judah and plunder King Jehoshaphat's wealth. After that, maybe the northern kingdom.

Jehoshaphat caught wind of the impending attack. It didn't take a Pythagoras to do the math. His army was like a sand-castle facing a large breaker. The kingdom of Judah would be swept away unless he got some very strong help.

Now, forget for the moment that you know the fairytale-like ending to the story. What would it have been like to be Jehoshaphat? Bearing down on him was a brutal death for himself, everyone he loved, and tens of thousands of his people.

And everyone was looking to him to do something to save them. That's pressure.

Jehoshaphat's options were limited. He might have tried to negotiate surrender. But that likely would have been refused. And even if accepted, it still probably would have meant his death and Judah's destruction.

He might have quickly sent a pile of money and promises of servitude to Syria or Egypt. But there really wasn't much time. Besides, he no doubt remembered his father Asa's costly mistake. As a younger king, Asa had cried out to the Lord for deliverance when his small army faced one million Ethiopian soldiers and God had miraculously answered him (2 Chronicles 14). But in later years, Asa abandoned that trust and forged an alliance with Syria. And God disciplined him severely for it (2 Chron. 16:1–10).

The wonderful thing about Jehoshaphat was that he really did trust the Lord and believe his promises. He did believe God could rescue Judah. He wanted to honor God by his trust. And, in this case, he didn't have many alternatives. Sometimes that is a great mercy.

So Jehoshaphat gathered the people of Judah in Jerusalem for a fast. They stood before the temple and the king, in an act of great leadership, pleaded their case before the Lord and then said: "We are powerless against this great horde that is coming against us. We do not know what to do, but our eyes are on you" (v. 12).

Isn't that a beautiful confession? It is so childlike in its humility and faith. It is, in fact, another Old Testament picture of the gospel. We are powerless to save ourselves. But when we look to God and call on him for deliverance from the impending judgment, he brings about a salvation beyond our wildest imagination.

The reason God orchestrated Jehoshaphat's predicament

is the same as his design in the tribulations and crises in our lives: he wants us to increasingly find freedom from fear.

You see, real freedom is not liberty to do what we want or the absence of distress. Real freedom is the deep-seated confidence that God really will provide *everything* we need. The person who believes this is the freest of all persons on earth, because no matter what situation he finds himself in, he has nothing to fear.

But the only way for sinners like us, with a bent toward unbelief in God, to find this kind of freedom is by experiencing repeatedly God's delivering power and his faithfulness. That's why we are "to count it all joy . . . when we meet trials of various kinds" (James 1:2). These trials are making us free.

God answered Jehoshaphat's faith-filled prayer in a spectacular way. He threw the armies of Ammon, Moab, and Edom into confusion, and they slaughtered one another. Jehoshaphat and his choir-led army never had to lift a sword. And it took them three days to carry the plunder back home.

God's word to you through this story, in all the crises you face, is this: "Do not be afraid and do not be dismayed at this great horde, for the battle is not yours but God's" (2 Chron. 20:15).

"Therefore I tell you, her sins, which are many, are forgiven—for she loved much. But he who is forgiven little, loves little."

LUKE 7:47

14

WHAT LOVE FOR GOD LOOKS LIKE

Luke 7:36–50

HE HAD THE HOLY One of Israel (Isa. 54:5) in his house, reclining at his table. The Prophet that Moses had foretold (Deut. 18:15) was sharing dinner with him. The Lord of glory, the Resurrection and the Life (John 11:25), was speaking with him face-to-face. The great climactic moment of history he claimed to be living for had arrived. It should have been a deliriously wonderful, breathtaking honor for Simon to host the Messiah.

But Simon was not amazed. As he looked at Jesus, all he saw was a dusty Nazarene whose claims could be interpreted as, well, delusional.

And Jesus's feet were still dirty. Offering foot washing to guests had been a deeply ingrained custom for Near Eastern peoples for thousands of years. To not offer it was to dishonor one's guest. It's not likely that Simon simply forgot.

But Jesus showed no sign of offense. And with the meal on the table, superficial pleasantries were exchanged. A few polite questions were asked.

Suddenly all eyes facing Jesus were filled with confused concern, focused toward his feet. Jesus looked back.

A woman was standing near him, clearly not part of the

household. She was looking intensely at him, cradling a small jar in her hands. She began to sob and dropped to her knees. And as her tears flowed, she leaned over and let them drop on Jesus's soiled feet and wiped them off, along with the dirt, with her hair.

Then she kissed Jesus's feet.

Gasps and murmurs were heard around the table. This woman had a reputation known to all the local guests. It was improper even to speak openly about what had given her this reputation. She was simply called a "sinner." Everyone knew what was packed into that word.

So everyone was mortified by her clearly inappropriate, even intimate contact. Except, apparently, Jesus. He did not seem shocked. And he did nothing to stop her.

An alarmed servant moved toward the woman but Simon waved him off. This was a revealing moment.

As Simon watched the woman pour fragrant oil from her jar on Jesus's feet, he felt both contempt and pleasure. His appraisal of Jesus was being vindicated before his eyes. Nothing spoke more eloquently of the falseness of this so-called prophet than his stunning lack of discernment regarding this immoral woman. No holy man would have let her pollute him with her touch. He began to rehearse what he would report to the Council.

"Simon, I have something to say to you." Jesus's words snapped Simon's attention back. "Say it, Teacher," he replied.

"A certain moneylender had two debtors. One owed five hundred denarii, and the other fifty. When they could not pay, he cancelled the debt of both. Now which of them will love him more?"

Simon answered, "The one, I suppose, for whom he cancelled the larger debt." And Jesus said to him, "You have judged rightly."

Then turning toward the woman Jesus said to Simon, "Do you see this woman? I entered your house; you gave me no water for my feet, but she has wet my feet with her tears and wiped them with her hair. You gave me no kiss, but from the time I came in she has not ceased to kiss my feet. You did not anoint my head with oil, but she has anointed my feet with ointment. Therefore I tell you, her sins, which are many, are forgiven—for she loved much."

Then looking back, penetratingly into Simon's eyes, Jesus said, "But he who is forgiven little, loves little." A shocked silence hung in the air.

And then with tender authority Jesus spoke to the woman: "Your sins are forgiven. Your faith has saved you; go in peace."

○ ○

As a Pharisee, Simon enjoyed a reputation as a godly man. He had significant theological education, had memorized extensive portions of Scripture, exercised rigorous self-discipline, prayed religiously, and tithed meticulously. The sorts of things men admire.

The woman's reputation was sleazy. Her law breaking was public knowledge. No one mistook her as a servant of God. Though men had desired her, no one admired her.

Yet in front of all the dinner party guests, Jesus declared that the debauched woman actually loved God much, while the ritually clean Pharisee loved God little. Why? Simply because the woman believed that she desperately needed the forgiveness Jesus offered in his gospel, while Simon did not.

"He who is forgiven little, loves little." This little sentence reveals a mammoth truth for us: we will love God to the degree that we recognize the magnitude of our sins and the immensity of God's grace to forgive them.

That is what Jesus is looking for. This is the kind of worshipers the Father is seeking (John 4:23).

For at its essence, true worship is a passionate love for God, not moralistic rule keeping or feats of self-discipline. For sinners like us, the fuel of that love is a profound realization, in the words of former slave trader-turned-pastor, John Newton, "that I am a great sinner, and that Christ is a great Saviour."[1]

---

[1] As quoted in Jonathan Aitken, *John Newton: From Disgrace to Amazing Grace* (Wheaton, IL: Crossway, 2007), 347.

But when he saw the wind, he was afraid, and beginning to sink he cried out, "Lord, save me." Jesus immediately reached out his hand and took hold of him, saying to him, "O you of little faith, why did you doubt?"

MATTHEW 14:30-31

15

WHEN A ROCK SUNK SLOWLY

PETER AND FAITH

Matthew 14:13–33 and John 6:1–21

THE DAY HAD BEEN another mind-blower for the disciples.

As they rowed toward Capernaum, it was hard to stop talking about what they had seen. Five thousand men, plus women and children, and Jesus had fed them all! With one boy's lunch! The power Jesus commanded both thrilled and unnerved them.

And they had felt the heady momentum of surging public support when the massive picnic turned into a "Jesus for king" rally. The people had begun to understand! The Messiah had arrived! The kingdom was beginning to emerge right before their eyes.

And then it had all ended so strangely. Surprisingly, Jesus was visibly disturbed by the crowd's enthusiasm, and he moved quickly to douse it with hard, confusing words. The people's support soured to disillusionment.

Jesus could be so hard to figure out.

And why had he been in such a hurry for them to get to Capernaum that he had them row by night? And why were they to leave without him? They had taken the last boat on the shore. If Jesus intended to join them in Capernaum by morning, it was going to be one whale of a walk.

Then the wind picked up and the waves grew stronger,

pushing against every pull of the oars. This was going to add hours to the trip. Adrenaline-fueled discussion was replaced by fatigue-fueled irritability. One of them commented that at this speed, Jesus would probably beat them there on foot.

Just then another shouted, "What's that?" All eyes strained sternward. A form was approaching in the murky dark. Peter stood up on the small rear deck and looked hard. It could not possibly be what it looked like. But soon it was unmistakable. Someone—or something—was walking toward them across the water! An unearthly fear seized the men. One spoke in a hushed panic: "It is a ghost!" The rowers found new energy.

But a familiar voice called to them, "Take heart; it is I. Do not be afraid."

Jesus? It sounded like Jesus. But he was *walking on top of the water!* Maybe a spirit could do that, but not a human! Peter motioned to the rowers to stop. It *was* Jesus. Mouths hung open, but no one had words.

Except Peter. "Lord, if it is you, command me to come to you on the water." Every astonished face turned to Peter. No one else had even thought of that yet. Jesus responded, "Come."

So Peter sat on the gunwale, swung his legs over the side, and carefully put his weight on what should have engulfed him. Then he stood up. There was a collective gasp from the boat. One degree of surreal to another. Then he began to take tentative steps toward Jesus. The others held their breath.

Suddenly Peter froze. He looked down at the waves drenching his legs. There was panic in his eyes. Then he began to sink, as if into mud. He reached out toward Jesus and cried, "Lord, save me!" Jesus stepped forward, reached out, grabbed his arm, and pulled him up. Peter, looking intensely at Jesus was breathing hard.

Jesus said to him with affectionate firmness, "O you of little faith, why did you doubt?"

○ ○

Peter showed remarkable faith in asking to follow Jesus out on to the water. No one else did.

But when he began walking, what held him up? We might quickly assume it was his faith. But that's not accurate. Peter's faith wasn't keeping him afloat. Jesus was. Peter knew that. That's why he didn't just leap out of the boat on his own. He asked Jesus to command him to come. What Jesus did was honor Peter's faith by commanding the water to bear his weight.

Lesson 1: Faith is not faith in our faith in Jesus, it's faith in the power of Jesus's word.

But once Peter was outside the safety of the boat, on uncharted waters, everything started feeling precarious. Why? Well, because people don't actually *walk* on water. We may be so familiar with the story that the ridiculousness of walking on water doesn't strike us. But it struck Peter at that moment.

And he started to sink.

But have you ever noticed that Peter the Rock didn't sink like a rock? The last time you jumped into a pool, how gradually did you sink? There's something profound going on here. Peter began to sink when his faith shifted from the firmness of Jesus's word to the instability of his circumstance. And when he did, it was Jesus letting him sink—slowly. And for Peter that was a grace.

Why? Because Peter's sinking produced his cry to Jesus. It quickly got Peter to stop looking to the world or himself as the source of truth and salvation and got his focus back on his Savior. When he did that, Jesus pulled him back up.

Lesson 2: Jesus's word is truer and stronger than what we see or feel, and when we doubt that, sometimes he graciously lets us sink to help us refocus.

Trusting in Jesus and his word over our perceptions is difficult to learn. That's why the Lord takes us through so many different faith-testing, faith-building experiences.

And when he does, it is never for just our own benefit. He's displaying his power so others' faith will be strengthened too. And, like the rest of the disciples once Jesus and Peter were back in the boat, we end up saying to the Lord, "Truly you are the Son of God" (Matt. 14:33).

Jesus . . . marveled at him, and turning to the crowd that followed him, said, "I tell you, not even in Israel have I found such faith."

LUKE 7:9

16

FAITH THAT MAKES JESUS MARVEL

THE CENTURION AND FAITH

Luke 7:1–10

JESUS, THE "FOUNDER AND perfecter of our faith" (Heb. 12:2), once marveled at the great faith he found in a man. And it's the only instance recorded in the Gospels when Jesus responded that way. Who was this man? A rabbi? No. A disciple? Nope. A Roman soldier.

○ ○

Jesus had walked down from the brow of the low mountain outside of Capernaum, his adopted home (Matt. 4:13). He had just delivered what would become the most famous sermon in history.

When Jesus entered the town, he was met by a group of Jewish elders. They had an urgent request. Would Jesus come quickly to the home of a Roman centurion whose servant was so ill he was near death? The centurion himself had sent these elders to Jesus to make this request.

This was strange. Jewish leaders were not in the habit of being fond of Roman soldiers.

Feeling the obvious oddness of the request, one of the elders quickly added, "He is worthy to have you do this for him, for he loves our nation, and he is the one who built us our synagogue."

This was also strange. Roman soldiers were not in the habit of being fond of Jews.

Jesus discerned the Father's direction in this and so he set off with them to the centurion's home. He had also just been preaching on the importance of loving one's enemies. This was something to encourage.

As they neared the house, another group of men intercepted them. They huddled in a brief, hushed conference with the confused elders. Some observers figured it was too late.

Then a representative of the interceptors stepped over to Jesus and said respectfully, "Teacher, I have a message for you from my Roman friend. He says,

> Lord, do not trouble yourself, for I am not worthy to have you come under my roof. Therefore I did not presume to come to you. But say the word, and let my servant be healed. For I too am a man set under authority, with soldiers under me: and I say to one, "Go" and he goes; and to another, "Come," and he comes; and to my servant, "Do this," and he does it.

A murmur wove through the crowd. He didn't want Jesus to come.

Jesus's eyes held the man's as he pondered the profound words. From a Roman soldier.

> Who has believed what he has heard from us?
>   And to whom has the arm of the LORD been revealed?
>   (Isa. 53:1)

Jesus's mouth eased into a smile. He shook his head slightly.

> For that which has not been told them they see,
>   and that which they have not heard they understand.
>   (Isa. 52:15)

This emissary of Israel's enemy understood what even these Jewish elders didn't grasp. He looked at the elders.

> The stone that the builders rejected
>> has become the cornerstone.
> This is the LORD's doing;
>> it is marvelous in our eyes. (Ps. 118:22–23)

Then he turned to his disciples and the small crowd that had followed him off the mountain and said in a loud voice, "I tell you, not even in Israel have I found such faith" (v. 9).

○ ○

Jesus "marveled" at this man's faith. When Jesus marvels, we must meditate.

Luke chose the Greek word *thaumazo* (thou-mad'-zo), which we translate "marveled" or "amazed," to describe Jesus's response to the centurion's faith.[1] The only other time this word is used to describe Jesus's response to someone else's faith is in Mark 6:6, when he marvels at the *lack of faith* in the people of Nazareth, those who knew him best.

It is a gospel irony that the only person recorded in the Gospels whose faith made Jesus marvel was a Roman soldier. The only reason he was in Palestine was to help keep the Jews under the domineering rule of the pagan Tiberius.

It amazed Jesus that a Gentile soldier of all people, a stranger to the covenant, a man with limited understanding of the Scriptures at best, saw what few of the covenant people saw when they looked at Jesus: the Son of God. Jewish crowds flocked around Jesus. Jewish leaders lobbied and debated him. But like Peter in the boat full of fish (Luke 5:7–8), the Centurion recognized divine holiness in Jesus and sinfulness in himself and knew he was not worthy of Jesus's presence.

---

[1] Matthew also chooses this word in Matthew 8:10.

He also recognized Jesus's authority. While Jewish elders asked Jesus questions like, "By what authority are you doing these things, and who gave you this authority?" (Matt. 21:23), this foreigner knew exactly who Jesus was. He knew Jesus had authority from the Father to command the natural world. He knew proximity was no factor. Jesus could speak disease out of existence from any distance.

And Jesus marveled that in this Centurion he saw a first-fruit and foreshadow of what he had come to bring about: that "many [would] come from east and west and recline at table with Abraham, Isaac, and Jacob in the kingdom of heaven" (Matt. 8:11).

This man whose faith made Jesus marvel was not a disciple, did no miracles, planted no churches, had no degree, and no religious title. His spiritual résumé was unimpressive. The man with the greatest faith in Israel was a centurion who simply knew who Jesus was, what he was able to do, humbly asked him, and trusted that he would receive what he needed.[2] He really believed in Jesus.

That is still the faith that makes Jesus marvel.

---

[2] "And whatever you ask in prayer, you will receive, if you have faith" (Matt. 21:22).

For the sake of Christ, then, I am content with weaknesses, insults, hardships, persecutions, and calamities. For when I am weak, then I am strong.

2 CORINTHIANS 12:10

17

ARE YOU CONTENT WITH WEAKNESSES?

PAUL AND HUMILITY

2 Corinthians 11–12

EVERY DAY, AS WE seek to follow Jesus, we deal with incessant weaknesses in our bodies, emotions, relationships, families, vocations, and churches. We are "beset with weakness" (Heb. 5:2). And they tempt us to discouragement, sometimes exasperation.

But one of the precious gifts of 2 Corinthians is that, through Paul, God teaches us a great gospel paradox of the life of faith: God's grace is more clearly seen and more deeply savored in our weaknesses than in our strengths.

○○

Paul was deeply concerned for the Corinthian church. "Super-apostles" had found their way to Corinth. They were parasitic charlatans who had followed in Paul's wake and were now maligning him.

So Paul wrote this letter. But his primary concern was not his reputation. He wrote because these men were siphoning glory from God and imperiling the Corinthians by distorting the gospel. And they were discrediting Paul in order to inflate their self-importance. This forced Paul to call out these imposters and contrast their doctrine, character, and labors with his own.

But it was tortuous for him. In defending himself it felt like he was "talking like a madman" (2 Cor. 11:23). Reluctantly, Paul listed revelations he had received, ways he had suffered for the sake of the gospel and the churches, and how he had never personally benefitted financially from the Corinthians.

Why was Paul so reluctant to talk about these things? It was far more than self-conscious awkwardness. Paul was very concerned that in drawing attention to his giftings, experiences, and endurance he might obscure the grace of God—he might do just what the "super-apostles" were doing. Boasting about himself was dangerous.

How dangerous? Test yourself. When you read in 2 Corinthians of Paul's lashings, beatings, imprisonments, shipwrecks, danger, hunger, exposure, and mind-blowing revelations, what are you tempted to think? Do you compare yourself to him? Do you look at his faith, brains, courage, tenacity, and work ethic and think, "Next to Paul I'm one sorry Christian"?

That is a danger Paul feared. Because when that happens, we usually look away from Christ, stop trusting in the sufficiency of his grace, and look to how our own experiences and achievements compare with others' as the basis for our acceptance with God.

Our fallen natures crave self-glory. We seek the admiration of others. We love the myth of the superhero because we want to be one. So we want our successes and strengths to be known and our failures and weaknesses hidden. And since strong, competent, high achievers earn human admiration, we are tempted to believe that they impress God in a similar way.

That's the last thing Paul wants us to believe. Paul knew better than most that it is not human achievements that showcase the grace of God. It is human helplessness.

For all his attainments, Paul viewed himself as the foremost of sinners (1 Tim. 1:15). Apart from God's grace in giving him the free gift of Christ's righteousness, all of Paul's achievements were "rubbish" (Phil. 3:8–9). Paul knew the impotence of self-righteousness (Phil. 3:6–9). He knew who had brought him to faith (Acts 9:5), called him to be an apostle (Rom. 1:1), sent him to make Gentile disciples (Rom. 1:5), and called him to suffer for his sake (Acts 9:16). Yes, Paul knew that he worked harder than just about everybody. But he knew that it was not him, but the grace of God that was with him (1 Cor. 15:10).

And one reason he knew this so profoundly was that Jesus had disciplined him. Knowing how Paul's indwelling sin might respond to the power and fruitfulness he would experience, Jesus gifted him with a "thorn in the flesh," a "messenger of Satan" to harass him (2 Cor. 12:7). It would be a continual reminder to Paul that he depended on Jesus for everything.

Don't you love the power and wisdom of God? He enlisted a messenger of Satan to serve Paul! It must have been maddening to the demons. Jesus knows how to "put them to open shame" (Col. 2:15).

But like us, Paul didn't immediately recognize the thorn as a gift. He pleaded for deliverance. But Jesus replied, "My grace is sufficient for you, for my power is made perfect in weakness" (2 Cor. 12:9).

This opened up a world of insight to Paul. God showing his strength through weak things was laced all through redemptive history, culminating in the cross.

That's why Paul said, "If I must boast, I will boast of the things that show my weakness" (2 Cor. 11:30). He even went beyond that: "For the sake of Christ, then, I am *content* with weaknesses, insults, hardships, persecutions, and calamities. For when I am weak, then I am strong" (2 Cor. 12:10).

○ ○

Like he did for Paul, the Lord has assigned certain weaknesses to you. Are you content with them?

By weaknesses I don't mean sin: "Let not sin therefore reign in your mortal body, to make you obey its passions" (Rom. 6:12). Neither do I mean foolishness: "Like a dog that returns to his vomit is a fool who repeats his folly" (Prov. 26:11).

But we all have different kinds of constitutional limitations, illnesses, and disabilities ("weaknesses"), and circumstantial adversity ("insults, hardships, persecutions, and calamities"). All of them make us groan. They seem at first like joy-stealers. Yet what God wants us to know through this text is that he has given them to us for our *joy*—yes, our joy—even if it's Satan harassing us.

Here's the secret: the more aware you are of God's grace, the more humble, prayerful, thankful, patient, gracious, content, and joyful you will be. And you are more aware of God's grace when you are weak than when you are strong.

God will use the strengths he has given you. He certainly used Paul's strengths. But if it's contentment in God that you long for, then thank God for your weaknesses. Because it is through them that you and others will really know that God's grace is sufficient for you.

And behold, a leper came to him and knelt before him, saying, "Lord, if you will, you can make me clean." And Jesus stretched out his hand and touched him, saying, "I will; be clean." And immediately his leprosy was cleansed.

MATTHEW 8:2-3

18

ASK!

THE LEPER AND PROVISION

Matthew 8:1–4

HE WAS ONE OF the walking dead. It had almost been three years since the priest examined that suspicious spot on his left arm and looked at him with sympathy. "I'm so sorry. It's leprosy. May God have mercy on you, my son."

Leprosy made you die many times before it killed you. It cut you off from those you loved most in the world. It forced you to live with other unclean people in a hopeless colony away from the town. Those with more advanced cases showed you what you had to look forward to.

It also forced you to scream, "Unclean!" whenever people approached and suffer the humiliation of watching them cover themselves and hurry by, cutting you a wide swath. And worst of all, it excluded you from the worshiping community that once had been the center of your life.

He had once prayed that God would protect him from this disease. Then he had prayed that God would heal him. God had done neither.

What had he done to deserve leprosy? It must have been some sin. But it didn't make sense. He knew others who were living in sin and were perfectly healthy. He was confused and increasingly despondent.

Then news reached him that the rabbi Jesus was in the area. Word was that Jesus's teaching was controversial. But apparently he had healed sick people in Capernaum—some of them lepers. This was worth checking out.

So he joined the crowd on the mountain, keeping his distance, to listen to the rabbi teach and see if the healing stories were true.

What he heard transformed him. Jesus was different—from everyone. He spoke with power and authority. It was as if his very words coursed with life. He talked about the kingdom of God and the end of death and the promise of eternal life. And Jesus claimed that he could grant it!

Normally he would have written Jesus off as another delusional "messiah." A dying man didn't have time for delusions. Yet here he was, hanging on Jesus's words.

Maybe it was because Jesus wasn't just talk. People he knew as sinners repented and received forgiveness. Demon-possessed people received deliverance. And diseased people received healing.

But it was more than that. The joy his followers had seemed to go deeper than good health. They were clean inside. They were free. He wasn't sure what it was, but the hope he tasted in Jesus's words made him long for something more than healing.

So he made up his mind. Whatever it took, he was going to get to Jesus and ask him to cleanse him from his leprosy and anything else that defiled him. And if Jesus granted him this gift, he was going to follow him.

So he trailed Jesus down the mountain, looking and praying for the right moment. He had an anxious knot in his gut. What if the moment never came? What if it came and Jesus said no?

It came just as Jesus reached the bottom of the mountain. So he moved quickly and dropped on his knees before the rabbi and blurted out, "Lord, if you will, you can make me clean."

He amazed himself at the confidence with which he said those words.

Jesus looked at him. It seemed like a long time. All the conversation nearby stopped. The man could feel everyone watching. Then the kindest smile he'd ever seen spread across Jesus's face as he stretched out his hand and touched him. "I will; be clean."

The first thing he felt was Jesus's mercy. He had not been touched by a nonleper in three years.

Then he felt heat course through his whole body. Then tingling! He felt tingling in the tips of his fingers—fingers he had thought would never feel again! There were gasps from the crowd. He pulled up his sleeves. No spots! He looked up at Jesus with stunned, speechless joy. He knew he was clean.

Jesus helped him stand up and firmly instructed him to tell no one, but to go show himself to the priest with the gift commanded by Moses "for a proof to them." Nodding, the man stammered, "Thank you!" And with another smile Jesus was off.

As the former leper walked toward the temple, Jesus's words were ringing in his ears: "I will; be clean." He shivered. "I will." Jesus *wanted* to grant him what he asked for. "Be clean." Jesus had the *power* to do it.

That morning all he had wanted was to be healed of leprosy. But now it seemed like that was just a prelude to something much bigger.

○ ○

What is it that you want? Jesus's word to you is, "Ask, and it will be given to you; seek, and you will find; knock, and it will be opened to you. For everyone who asks receives, and the one who seeks finds, and to the one who knocks it will be opened" (Luke 11:9–10). "Fear not, little flock, for it is your Father's good pleasure to give you the kingdom" (Luke 12:32).

It is true, "No good thing does he withhold from those who walk uprightly" (Ps. 84:11). Sometimes the good thing is healing. Sometimes the good thing is affliction so that we know more profoundly just how sufficient God's grace is for us (2 Cor. 12:9). But even if healing is delayed, it will come.

With all his heart God looks forward to giving us the kingdom in full. Then "he will swallow up death forever; and the Lord God will wipe away tears from all faces, and the reproach of his people he will take away from all the earth" (Isa. 25:8). For "he who did not spare his own Son but gave him up for us all, how will he not also with him graciously give us all things?" (Rom. 8:32).

So ask! God is willing, able, and determined to give you the very best.

"I am the resurrection and the life. Whoever believes in me, though he die, yet shall he live, and everyone who lives and believes in me shall never die. Do you believe this?"

JOHN 11:25-26

19

"DO YOU BELIEVE THIS?"

MARTHA AND DEATH

John 11:1–44

"NOW JESUS LOVED MARTHA and her sister and Lazarus. So, when he heard that Lazarus was ill, he stayed two days longer in the place where he was."

Can you bear these two sentences? The most loving thing Jesus could do at that moment was to let Lazarus die. But it didn't look or feel like love to Martha.

◯◯

"Martha, the Teacher has come. He's near the village."

Martha's emotions collided. Just hearing that Jesus was near resuscitated hope in her soul—the same hope she had felt the day she sent word for him to come.

But it was quickly smothered with grief and disappointment. Lazarus had died four days earlier. She had prayed desperately that Jesus would come in time. God had not answered her prayers. What could Jesus do now?

And yet . . . if anyone could do something, Jesus could. He had "the words of eternal life" (John 6:68). Martha hurried out.

When she saw Jesus, she could not restrain her grief and love. She collapsed at his feet and sobbed, "Lord, if you had been here, my brother would not have died."

Jesus laid his hand on her head.

He had come to Bethany to destroy the Devil's works (1 John 3:8). He had come to give death a taste of its coming final defeat (1 Cor. 15:26). He had come to show that now was the time when the dead would hear the voice of the Son of God, and those who heard would live (John 5:25).

Martha did not know all this. Neither did she know that what was about to happen would hasten Jesus's own death—a death that would purchase her resurrection and both of Lazarus's. She didn't know how this weighed on him, how great was his distress until it was accomplished (Luke 12:50).

But Jesus's wordless kindness soothed her.

When Martha's sorrowful convulsion had passed she said, "But even now I know that whatever you ask from God, God will give you."

Jesus gently lifted Martha's eyes and looked at her with affectionate intensity. "Your brother will rise again."

His living words revived her hope. Could he mean . . . ? No. She dared not let herself hope that way. Not after four days.

"I know that he will rise again in the resurrection on the last day."

Yes. Lazarus would rise again on the last day. Martha had no idea how deeply Jesus longed for that day. But Jesus meant more than that.

He replied, "I am the resurrection and the life. Whoever believes in me, though he die, yet shall he live, and everyone who lives and believes in me shall never die. Do you believe this?"

The power with which Jesus spoke caused faith to swell in Martha's soul. She wasn't sure what this all meant, but as he spoke, it was as if death itself was being swallowed up (1 Cor. 15:54). "No one ever spoke like this man" (John 7:46).

She answered, "Yes, Lord; I believe that you are the Christ, the Son of God, who is coming into the world."

○ ◎

We know how the story ends. But in the horrible days of Lazarus's agonizing illness and in the dark misery of the days following his death, Martha did not know what God was doing. He seemed silent and unresponsive. Jesus didn't come. It's likely that she knew word had reached him. She was confused, disappointed, and overwhelmed with grief.

And yet, Jesus delayed precisely *because* he loved Martha and Mary and Lazarus. He knew that Lazarus's death and resurrection would give maximum glory to God, and his friends would all experience maximum joy in that glory. It would make all their suffering seem light and momentary (2 Cor. 4:17).

God only ordains our deep disappointment and profound suffering for the sake of far greater joy in the glory he will reveal to us (Rom. 8:18). It is crucial to remind one another of this. Before we know what Jesus is doing, circumstances can look all wrong. And we are tempted to interpret God's apparent inaction as unloving, when in fact God is loving us in the most profound way he possibly can.

So in your anguish of soul, hear Jesus ask with strong affection, "Do you believe this?" (John 11:26).

Simon Peter said to them, "I am going fishing." They said to him, "We will go with you." They went out and got into the boat, but that night they caught nothing.

JOHN 21:3

20

WHEN YOU AREN'T SURE WHAT TO DO NEXT

PETER AND WAITING

John 21:1–14

"I AM GOING FISHING."

Peter didn't know what else to do. The past few weeks had been indescribably intense with the nightmare of Jesus's crucifixion and the ineffable wonder of his resurrection.

Now he was sitting with Thomas, Nathanael, James, John, and two others. They were just waiting. It was disorienting. Jesus wasn't there and he hadn't told them what to do next.

Peter used to know just what to do: prepare the nets and boat, go fishing, take what he caught and sell it in the market. Fishing was hard and sometimes dangerous work. But Peter knew what was expected of him. The memory of the familiar was comforting.

So as long as he didn't know what else to do, he figured he might as well do something productive. The others replied, "We will go with you." Peter wasn't the only restless one.

All night they fished. Cast and pull. Nothing. Cast and pull. Nothing. Try the other side of the boat. Nothing. Move the boat. Nothing. A little deeper. Nothing. A little shallower. Nothing. Where are the fish? Nothing. Whose idea was this? There may have been a sharp word or two.

Just as day was breaking, they heard a voice from the shore. "Children, do you have any fish?" James's exasperated response was, "No!" "Cast your net on the right side of the boat, and you will find some."

Ordinarily this would have been irritating. They didn't recognize the speaker, but his instructions were familiar. This had happened before (Luke 5:1–11). Peter and John glanced at one another and then tossed the net. The sudden weight almost pulled them overboard. It couldn't be! It was! Fish! And they were huge! They couldn't even get the net into the boat.

John's eyes were as big as the fish when he looked at Peter and said, "It is the Lord!" Peter handed the net to Nathanael, threw on his outer garment, and dove into the sea, leaving the others to drag the bulging net.

When they got to shore, they found Jesus preparing breakfast for them. He already had fish! Graciously, and perhaps with an affectionate tease, he said, "Bring some of the fish that *you* have just caught." Then he served them breakfast.

And *then* Jesus gave Peter the next instructions.

○ ○

This is vintage Jesus, always graciously leading and serving his bewildered disciples. And since we twenty-first-century disciples are just as easily bewildered, it's good for us to remember some helpful principles from this story.

First, waiting on Jesus is a common experience for disciples. Sometimes we wait for direction. Sometimes we're stuck in a very hard place and wait for release. Sometimes we wait to understand his purposes. Sometimes we wait for his provision. Jesus's timing and purposes are not always clear to us, though they are always best for us. So he wants our faith resting on the rock of his Word and not on the sand of our circumstance.

Second, when we're not sure what to do next, as Elisabeth Elliot says, "do the next thing."[1] No doubt the disciples had prayed for guidance during those days but no clear instructions had come yet. Fishing just seemed like a good idea. As it turned out, it was exactly what the Lord wanted them to do. Jesus *was* leading them, just differently. As they did the next thing, Jesus met them and directed them.

Third, Jesus is in complete control. Peter and his friends were experienced fishermen. They did their best, yet caught nothing. But that morning they discovered (again) that Jesus was sovereign over their decisions, the boat, the sea, the fish, and time.

Fourth, Jesus is always serving us, even when we can't see it. He serves us in every conceivable way: from paying for our sins (Heb. 2:17), to calling us as disciples (John 15:16), to ordering the fish we catch (Matt. 4:19), to serving us breakfast on the beach (Phil. 4:19), and bringing us to our eternal home (2 Tim. 4:18). Jesus loves to work for those who wait for him (Isa. 64:4).

In following Jesus there are seasons of bewildering intensity and seasons of bewildering waiting. He does not want us to panic during either. He is in control of both. When you don't understand his ways, trust his Word.

And when you're not sure what to do next, do the next thing.

---

[1] Elisabeth Elliot spoke and wrote on this topic in numerous places, but a helpful summary of her thoughts can be found at Back to the Bible, "Do the Next Thing," http://www.backtothebible.org/index.php/Gateway-to-Joy/Do-the-Next-Thing.html.

"Simon, son of John, do you love me?" . . . "Feed my sheep."

JOHN 21:17

21

JESUS CHOOSES AND USES FAILURES

PETER AND RESTORATION

John 21:15–19

"**SIMON, SON OF JOHN,** do you love me?"

Peter was grieved. Sitting on the beach after breakfast, Jesus had just asked him for the third time if he loved him. Peter had already wholeheartedly answered yes twice. What else was he supposed to say?

With these questions, the Lord was putting his finger on a very tender wound in Peter's heart. Peter's failure on the night of Jesus's trial had been simply horrible. In the hour of his Lord's greatest anguish, Peter had denied even knowing him. This sin shook Peter to the core of his being.

Jesus had told him that he would do it (John 13:38). But in the upper room, over the Passover meal, with his fellow disciples around him, Peter did not believe it. He could still hear himself proclaim, "I will lay down my life for you" (John 13:37).

He had had no idea how weak he really was. He had imagined himself boldly standing before the Sanhedrin side by side with Jesus, come what may. But that night, as Jesus was doing that very thing, Peter couldn't even stand before a servant girl: "You also are not one of this man's disciples, are you?" He had completely caved: "I am not" (John 18:17).

I am not. Those words had kept Peter up at night. He was

supposed to be a rock (Matt. 16:18). That night he had crumbled into pieces. He was not who he thought he was. *So who am I?* Peter had never been less confident in himself.

So when Jesus questioned Peter's love for a third time that morning, Peter grieved that he might have lost the Savior's trust. He had failed. But he did love him. All he could do was appeal to Jesus's omniscience: "Lord, you know everything; you know that I love you."

And Jesus did. In fact, later Peter realized what Jesus had done in that painful conversation. He had not doubted Peter's love at all. Rather, he had allowed Peter to confess his love for every wretched denial he had made on that dreadful night. Jesus's grace was overwhelming.

And the Lord had a word for Peter. In the future there would be another opportunity to confess his love publicly in the face of great cost. And then he said, "Follow me."

○○

One of Peter's good friends later wrote, "For we all stumble in many ways" (James 3:2). This is very true.

The guilt of past failures and sins can haunt and inhibit us in many ways. Satan loves to bind us up with the chains of condemnation. But Jesus aims to set us completely free.

When Jesus chose us to be his disciples, he foresaw our future failures as sure as he foresaw Peter's. We may be surprised by our own depravity, but Jesus isn't. We may not want to believe that we could deny Jesus by engaging in a sin that contradicts everything we believe. But Jesus knows what is in us (John 2:25). That's why he exhorts us along with Peter to "watch and pray that you may not enter into temptation. The spirit indeed is willing, but the flesh is weak" (Matt. 26:41).

Jesus also prays for us. When we do fail, we must remember what Jesus said to Peter before his failure: "I have prayed for you that your faith may not fail. And when you have turned again, strengthen your brothers" (Luke 22:32). Peter was going to sin—miserably. But Jesus had prayed for him. And Jesus's prayer was stronger than Peter's sin, and it's stronger than our sin too. "He is able to save to the uttermost those who draw near to God through him, since he always lives to make intercession for them" (Heb. 7:25). And "if we confess our sins, he is faithful and just to forgive us our sins and to cleanse us from all unrighteousness" (1 John 1:9).

And Jesus is the great restorer of failures who repent. Jesus's word to Peter before his failure was, "When you have turned again [repented], strengthen your brothers." And there on the beach he again gave Peter the greatest invitation any of us can receive on earth: "Follow me." The failure was to be left behind. There was kingdom work to do, there was a hard death to endure, and there was eternal life to be relished.

Peter's failure did not define him. And ours will not define us. They are horrible, humbling stumbles along the path of following Jesus. And Jesus paid for them all on the cross. He has settled our accounts with the Father and given us guiltlessness as a free gift of his love.

The church of Jesus Christ is a fellowship of forgiven failures. In Peter, Jesus shows us how he can transform a failure into a rock of strength for his church. Empowered by the Spirit of his beloved Lord, Peter became a humble, encouraging, suffering, and persevering disciple of Jesus.

And he remains a bold ambassador of the gospel of forgiveness to the most miserable failures.

And Zechariah said to the angel, "How shall I know this? For I am an old man, and my wife is advanced in years." And the angel answered him, "I am Gabriel. I stand in the presence of God, and I was sent to speak to you and to bring you this good news. And behold, you will be silent and unable to speak until the day that these things take place, because you did not believe my words, which will be fulfilled in their time."

LUKE 1:18-20

22

WHEN A REBUKE BECAME A REWARD

ZECHARIAH AND UNBELIEF

Luke 1

WHAT MIGHT ZECHARIAH AND Elizabeth have talked about after their friends left the naming ceremony where Zechariah had miraculously regained his speech?

◦ ◦

"So . . . are you going to tell me?"

Elizabeth was ready to burst. She had waited nearly a year to hear what had happened in the temple.

Zechariah was looking adoringly at the infant boy lying on his lap. "Baby John, there's something you need to know about women. They always want the *details*!" Zechariah glanced up playfully at his wife.

"The Lord has freed your tongue, Zechariah. It *needs* some exercise. Out with it!"

In some ways being mute for ten months had made it easier. How does one even describe such things? The moment had been so sacred, and overwhelming.

"That day seems like a dream. I remember walking into the temple. I had a knot of joyful fear in my stomach. I had been chosen by the Lord to intercede for Israel in the Holy Place! I remember praying as I lit the incense. And then suddenly there was a man standing just to my right! I never saw him come. He was just there! I was so startled I nearly dropped the fire."

"The angel looked like a man?"

"Well . . . yes. I guess. But I've never seen any man like him. It's hard to explain."

"Did he have wings like the carvings?"

Zechariah paused. "This is going to sound strange, but I'm not sure. I remember him not looking anything like I'd imagined. But his appearance is less clear in my memory than the words he spoke—and how suddenly conscious I was of my sinfulness. I felt unclean."

"So what exactly did he say?"

"I was terrified. You know how we're warned. If priests offer unrighteous intercession we could be struck dead. And at that moment it didn't feel unjust. So the first thing he said was, 'Do not be afraid, Zechariah.' His words gave me strength."

Looking at his wife with tears, he went on, "Then he said, 'Your prayer has been heard, and your wife Elizabeth will bear you a son, and you shall call his name John.'" Husband and wife both sobbed in sorrow-laced joy.

"Liz, all those years of praying. I had stopped hoping. But God *heard*." Elizabeth just nodded with closed, tearful eyes.

Zechariah wiped his face and beamed at his son. "And you will have joy and gladness, and many will rejoice at his birth, for he will be great before the Lord.'"

"The angel said that?"

Zechariah nodded. "'And he must not drink wine or strong drink, and he will be filled with the Holy Spirit,'" and looking at Elizabeth he said, "even from his mother's womb.'" Both were thinking of Mary and of John's womb-leap over the Miracle she was carrying.

"'And he will turn many of the children of Israel to the

Lord their God, and he will go before him in the spirit and power of Elijah, to turn the hearts of the fathers to the children, and the disobedient to the wisdom of the just, to make ready for the Lord a people prepared.'"

"The prophecy!"

"Yes. The prophet Malachi. Liz, those were the last words that the Lord spoke to our people through a prophet. It's been four hundred years of silence. But now the Lord is loosing the prophetic tongue of Israel, beginning with this little boy. God is visiting us again, this time with the Messiah! And our John will be his forerunner. Who are we that God would allow us to be a part of this marvel?"

Neither spoke for a while.

Then Elizabeth asked, "Why did the angel make you mute?"

Zechariah sighed. "I'm a sinfully proud man, Liz. I've viewed myself as a man who believes God's word. I've lived by his law. I've felt contempt for doubters. Though I've never said it out loud, I've secretly thought that my faith would be greater than some of our prophets and kings if only God spoke directly to me as he did to them.

"Well, God showed me what I really am. You know what I said to the angel? 'How shall I know this? For I am an old man, and my wife is advanced in years.' I—who have taught many about Abraham and Sarah—I doubted God when he sent an *angel* to tell me that he's answering my prayer. Is there a greater fool?

"So the angel said, 'I am Gabriel. I stand in the presence of God, and I was sent to speak to you and to bring you this good news. And behold, you will be silent and unable to speak until the day that these things take place, because you did not believe my words, which will be fulfilled in their time.'

"God was very gracious to only take my words. He could have taken my life."

"The Lord is gracious, Zechariah. That *is* the name he gave our son."[1]

Zechariah smiled again at John. "Yes. Isn't it beautiful? God has taught me more about his grace these past ten months of silence than in all my years of talking. Even his rebuke has become a reward for me. It's *all* grace! I love the ways of God, Liz."

The humble father then held his son in the air. "And this boy will help us all see that Messiah is coming to show the tender mercy of our God in forgiving undeserving sinners—even proud, faithless old priests."

○○

God's grace toward his children is infused in *everything* he does for us, even when he chastens us. "God always turns his rebukes into rewards" for his own.[2]

---

[1] "John" is derived from the Hebrew name יוֹחָנָן *(Yochanan)* meaning "YAHWEH is gracious" (http://www.behindthename.com/name/john).

[2] This quote is from an excellent sermon by John Piper on the story of Zechariah titled, "Jesus Is the Horn of Salvation," Desiring God, December 14, 1980, http://www.desiringgod .org/resource-library/sermons/jesus-is-the-horn-of-salvation/.

For not even his brothers believed in him.

JOHN 7:5

23

HOPE FOR OUR BELOVED UNBELIEVERS

JESUS'S SIBLINGS AND EVANGELISM

John 7:5

DO YOU HAVE FAMILY members who do not believe in Jesus? If so, you are in good company. So did Jesus. And I think this is meant to give us hope.

According to the apostle John, "Not even his brothers believed in him." That's incredible. Those who had lived with Jesus for thirty years really did not know him. Not one of Jesus's brothers is mentioned as a disciple during his precrucifixion ministry. But after his resurrection and ascension, there they are in the upper room worshiping him as God (Acts 1:14).

Why didn't they believe? And what made them change?

The Bible doesn't answer the first question. But I'll bet it was difficult to have Jesus for a brother.

First, Jesus would have been without peer in intellect and wisdom. He was astounding temple rabbis by age twelve (Luke 2:42, 47). A sinful gifted sibling can be a hard act to follow. Imagine a perfect gifted sibling.

Second, Jesus's consistent and extraordinary moral character must have made him odd and unnerving to be around. His siblings would have grown increasingly self-conscious around

him, aware of their own sinful, self-obsessed motives and be-
havior, while noting that Jesus didn't seem to exhibit any himself. For sinners, that could be hard to live with.

Third, Jesus was deeply and uniquely loved by Mary and
Joseph. How could they not have treated him differently? They
knew he was the Lord. Imagine their extraordinary trust in
and deference to Jesus as he grew older. No doubt the siblings
would have perceived a dimension to the relationship between
the oldest child and their parents that was different from what
they experienced.

And when swapping family stories, it would have been
hard to match a star appearing at your brother's birth.

Jesus out-classed his siblings in every category. How could
anyone with an active sin nature not resent being eclipsed by
such a phenom-brother? Familiarity breeds contempt when
pride rules the heart.

More pain than we know must have been behind Jesus's
words, "A prophet is not without honor except in his home-
town and in his own household" (Matt. 13:57).

So as we assess the role our weak, stumbling witness plays
in our family members' unbelief, let's remember Jesus—not
even a perfect witness guarantees that loved ones will see and
embrace the gospel. We must humble ourselves and repent
when we sin. But let's remember that the god of this world
and indwelling sin is what blinds the minds of unbelievers
(2 Cor. 4:4).

The story of Jesus's brothers can actually give us hope for
our loved ones. At the time his brothers claimed that Jesus
was "out of his mind" (Mark 3:21), it must have appeared very
unlikely that they would ever become his disciples. But eventually they did! And not only followers, but also leaders and
martyrs in the early church. The God who said, "Let light shine
out of darkness," shone in their hearts "to give the light of the

knowledge of the glory of God in the face of [their brother], Jesus" (2 Cor. 4:6).

So take heart! Don't give up praying for unbelieving family members. Don't take their resistance as the final word. They may yet believe, and be used significantly in the kingdom.

And while they resist, or if they have died apparently unbelieving, we can trust them to the Judge of all the earth who will be perfectly just (Gen. 18:25). Jesus does not promise that every parent, sibling, or child of a Christian will believe, but he does painfully promise that some families will divide over him (Matt. 10:34–39). We can trust him when it happens.

It is moving to hear James refer to his brother as "our Lord Jesus Christ, the Lord of glory" (James 2:1). Can you imagine what this phrase meant for James? The Lord of glory had once slept beside him, ate at his dinner table, played with his friends, spoke to him like a brother, endured his unbelief, paid the debt of his sin, and then brought him to faith.

It may have taken twenty to thirty years of faithful, prayerful witness by the Son of God, but the miracle occurred: his brothers believed. May the Lord of glory grant the same grace to our beloved unbelievers.

It happened, late one afternoon, when David arose from his couch and was walking on the roof of the king's house, that he saw from the roof a woman bathing; and the woman was very beautiful.

2 SAMUEL 11:2

24

SUCCESS CAN BE PERILOUS

KING DAVID AND SELFISHNESS

2 Samuel 11–12

WE ARE NEVER MORE vulnerable to sin than when we are successful, admired by others, and prosperous, as King David tragically discovered.

○○

It was spring again. David once had loved warm, fragrant spring afternoons on the palace roof. But this year the scent of almond blossoms smelled like deep regret.

David had no desire to look toward Uriah's empty house. If only he had not looked that way a year ago. The memory throbbed with pain. His conscience had warned him to stop watching Bathsheba. But in his desire-induced inertia it had felt like he couldn't pull himself away.

What pathetic self-deception! Couldn't pull himself away. He would never have tolerated such a weak excuse in another man. If Nathan had unexpectedly shown up while he was leering, would he have pulled himself away? Oh yes! He wouldn't have risked his precious reputation!

But there on the roof alone he had lingered. And in those minutes, sinful indulgence metastasized into a wicked, ultimately lethal plan.

David wept. His sovereign, lustful selfishness had stripped a married woman of her honor, murdered her loyal, valiant husband, and killed his own innocent baby boy. Bathsheba was now left with a desolate, hollow sadness.

And he shuddered at the Lord's dark promise: "The sword shall never depart from your house" (2 Sam. 12:10). The destruction had not run its full course.

How had he come to this?

David thought back to those hard, harrowing years when Saul chased him around Horesh. How often had he felt desperate? Daily he had depended on God for survival. He had longed for escape and peace in those days. Now he viewed them as among the best of his life.

And then came the tumultuous, heady years of uniting Judah and Israel under his kingship and subduing their enemies. And it had all climaxed with God's almost unbelievable promise to establish David's throne forever.

Had a man ever been so blessed by God? Every promise to him had been kept. Everything David touched had flourished. Never had Israel as a nation been so spiritually alive, so politically stable, so wealthy, so militarily powerful.

And at the peak of this unprecedented prosperity, David had committed such heinous sin. Why? How could he have resisted so many temptations in dangerous, difficult days and then yield at the height of success?

Almost as soon as the question formed in his mind he knew the answer: pride. Monstrous, self-obsessed pride.

Honored by his God, a hero to his people, a terror to his enemies, surrounded by fawning assistants and overflowing affluence, the poisonous weed of self-worship had grown insidiously in David's heart. The lowly shepherd that God had plucked by sheer grace from Bethlehem's hills to serve as Israel's king had been eclipsed in his own mind by David the

Great, the savior of his nation—a man whose exalted status entitled him to special privileges.

David cupped his face in his hands as his shame washed over him again. Bathsheba's body had been nothing more than a special privilege he had decided to bestow on himself. And in so doing he had placed himself above God, his office, his nation, Uriah's honor and life, Bathsheba's welfare—everything. David had sacrificed everything to the idol of himself.

David fell on his face and wept again. And he poured out his broken, contrite heart to God.

But profound hope was woven into the deep remorse David felt. Knowing he deserved death, David marveled at and worshiped God for the unfathomable depths of mercy in the words "The LORD also has put away your sin; you shall not die" (2 Sam. 12:13). It took his breath away. This word, this news good beyond comprehension, had come before a single sacrifice had been offered.

This was love that surpassed knowledge (Eph. 3:19). Something miraculous was at work here, something much more powerful than horrific sin. David wasn't quite sure how it worked. But what he did know is that he wanted other transgressors to know the amazingly gracious ways of God (Ps. 51:13–14).

○ ○

The greatest enemy of our souls is the pathologically selfish pride at the core of our fallen natures. If we look deep enough, this is what we will find feeding the strong sinful cravings of our appetites.

And this is why prosperity can be so spiritually dangerous. We tend to see our need for God more clearly in adversity. But seasons of success can be our most perilous because we are so easily deceived into thinking more highly of ourselves than we ought to think (Rom. 12:3). Self-exalting pride is what leads us to usurp God's rightful rule. We must beware this danger that lurks in blessings.

And when we sin, we must run to and not avoid the throne of grace (Heb. 4:16). On this side of the cross we now know fully what David didn't: God put away our sin by placing it on himself. Only at the cross will we hear, "The Lord also has put away your sin; you shall not die" (2 Sam. 12:13). Ever.

Jesus said to Philip, "Where are we to buy bread, so that these people may eat?" He said this to test him, for he himself knew what he would do. Philip answered him, "Two hundred denarii worth of bread would not be enough for each of them to get a little." One of his disciples, Andrew, Simon Peter's brother, said to him, "There is a boy here who has five barley loaves and two fish, but what are they for so many?"

JOHN 6:5-9

25

MORE THAN ENOUGH

PHILIP AND PROVISION

Matthew 14:13–20; Mark 6:30–44;
Luke 9:10–17; John 6:1–14

PHILIP SET HIS BASKET load of bread fragments down on the grass. He straightened his tired back and scanned the huge crowd of happy, sated people. It was hard to absorb what had just happened.

Andrew dropped his basket beside Philip's, blew a sigh, and leaned on Philip's shoulder. "Well done, Philip! You fed them, just like Jesus instructed. But I'd say you overestimated the bread."

With a dazed laugh Philip answered, "No, I overestimated the cost! I thought the bread would bankrupt us. I think *you're* the one who actually got the food."

"True. But who knew that a boy's lunch would be more than enough for the biggest picnic in Israel?"

"How many loaves did he have?"

"Five."

"And how many loaves do you think we gave out?"

"I have no idea. I've never seen so much bread in my life. There are easily over five thousand people here." Andrew did a silent calculation. "Maybe twenty thousand?"

Philip just shook his head in amazement, "That's not even counting the fish."

"I know. It would have taken Peter and me weeks to haul in

that many fish. And as I was passing them out I got to thinking, where did all these fish come from?"

"Where'd they come from?"

"Well, the boy had two fish, right? We know where those fish came from. Some fisherman caught them, sold them in the market, the boy's mother bought them, prepared them, and sent them with him. But we must have passed out ten thousand fish! Philip, where did those fish come from? Nobody caught them, or sold them, or bought them. Nobody prepared them. They just appeared!"

Mystified, Philip replied, "I didn't even think about that."

Andrew pulled a fish fragment from his basket. "Look, this fish has eyes. It has gills and fins. It's a real fish! But did it ever swim? Did it ever use these eyes or fins? Did it ever *live*? Did God snatch it out of the sea, prepare it, and give it to Jesus a second before he handed it to us? Or did he just create it there on the spot?"

Philip looked down at his basket. "The same is true of this bread. Did God take it from a barley field somewhere in the world and instantly make it into bread, or did he speak it into existence fully baked?"

Both of them looked over at Jesus in wonder. Andrew said, "Whatever he did is beyond comprehension. Philip, we may have been the first to eat miracle food since the manna last fell in the wilderness."

Philip quoted Moses: "The LORD your God will raise up for you a prophet like me from among you, from your brothers—it is to him you shall listen" (Deut. 18:15).

Then turning to Andrew he said, "I've known he's the One from the time he first called me (John 1:45). I've seen him turn water into wine (John 2:1–11). I've seen healings like nothing I've ever heard of before. And yet, I'm so slow to listen; so slow to believe. When he asked me about feeding the crowd,

I didn't even think about his power to provide. I just looked at how little money we had and saw an impossibility. I'm no better than Moses's generation who saw miracle after miracle and then promptly forgot God's power the next time they faced an obstacle."

"I'm in the same boat with you, Philip. I'm the one who asked, 'What are five barley loaves and two fish for so many?'"

"Andrew, I don't want to forget this moment. He was able to make five loaves and two fish more than enough for five thousand people. He spoke provision into existence. This is why he's told us not to be anxious about our needs like food or clothing (Matt. 6:25) but to 'seek first the kingdom of God and his righteousness' believing that 'all these things will be added to' us (Matt. 6:33). Please remind me of this the next time something looks impossible."

○ ○

All four Gospels feature the feeding of the five thousand because God wants you to believe that he "is able to make all grace abound to you, so that having all sufficiency in all things at all times, you may abound in every good work" (2 Cor. 9:8). For if you really believe this, your worries are over.

"Rabbi, who sinned, this man or his parents, that he was born blind?" Jesus answered, "It was not that this man sinned, or his parents, but that the works of God might be displayed in him."

JOHN 9:2-3

26

GOD'S PURPOSES CAN BE OPPOSITE OF OUR PERCEPTIONS

THE MAN BORN BLIND AND SUFFERING

John 9

THERE HE SAT, THE scum of society, on the footstep of heaven on earth. A sorry piece of work begging the condescending mercy of pious passersby going in and out of the temple. Enough mercy today and he could eat.

This man was blind. He had been born that way. And it was his own fault. As a fetus this man had sinned in the womb against the Almighty. Either that or his parents had sinned and brought a curse upon him. Whichever it was, he was suffering a just punishment.

Those who had been righteous fetuses walked by and sometimes dropped a coin in his hand. This would merit them even more divine favor.

You see, in the Law and the Prophets, God had not explained exactly why one sinful person suffers more than another sinful person. So theologians had deduced that a person's suffering must result from specific, personal offenses against God.

Interestingly, Job's three friends (Job 2:11) had reached the same conclusions about Job's suffering. Only God had said to them, "You have not spoken of me what is right" (Job 42:8). He was poised to deliver a similar rebuke.

Jesus's disciples had learned from the theologians. But seeing the blind man on the temple steps triggered a question that had perplexed them. Fortunately, they had the singular honor of having God the Son, the fullness of deity dwelling bodily (Col. 2:9), walking with them so they could ask him.

"Rabbi, who sinned, this man or his parents, that he was born blind?"

God the Son stopped and looked at the man. Then he gave an answer that would turn their understanding on its head and affect the futures of millions: "It was not that this man sinned or his parents, but that the works of God might be displayed in him."

Can you hear the disciples catch their breath? Have you caught yours?

Let me restate what Jesus said: this man was blind because God *made* him blind in order to demonstrate his power in him (Ex. 4:11). His blindness had *nothing* to do with his or his parents' personal sin. The purpose of this man's disability was not punishment but proclamation. It's just that no one knew it until that day.

Jesus's answer was the dismantling of an oppressive theological system. It took the burden of blame for disability off the frail shoulders of the broken and placed it on the omnipotent shoulders of God. Men may wrestle with the problem with pain. When they do, let them strive with God, not the stricken.

And when Jesus spoke these words, he understood their full implications. They were ocean deep. Jesus knew what this moment of proclamation had cost in the currency of this man's pain.

All those years the man and his parents had labored under a perception that God had brought his judgment upon them for an unknown reason. All those years they had borne other people's contempt. Imagine what the man's childhood must have been like. Imagine the insults he endured, the indignities, the injuries, the poverty, the loneliness, and the isolation from other children. How many hours did he weep? How many pleas for mercy did he pray? No hope for an education. No hope for marriage. He had one vocational option: begging. His life had been very hard.

And, according to Jesus, this was God's plan. Was it worth it? We shall see, if God wills.

After his world-shaking statement, Jesus spat on the ground, made mud with his saliva, put the mud on the man's eyes, and said, "Go, wash in the pool of Siloam" (v. 7). The man went, washed, and came back *seeing*!

In that moment everything changed. Oh the power of the Word! Light shown into dark eyes. A brain that had never processed optical stimuli was given immediate ability to interpret a visual world.

But even more revolutionary in its repercussions, the man went from being perceived as the object of God's wrath to being the object of God's kindness! Those who had always believed he was "born in utter sin" (v. 34) now discovered that God had made him blind in order to show mercy to him and pronounce judgment on self-righteous religious people. "For judgment I came into this world, that those who do not see may see, and those who see may become blind" (v. 39).

So was it worth it—suffering so much for decades in order to proclaim the glory of God's grace? It all depends on what God gave him in return. God so loved him that he gave his only Son so that by believing in him, this man would not perish but have eternal life (John 3:16). What this man received beyond his miraculous physical healing was the far more miraculous forgiveness of all his sins (Matt. 9:5–8) and eternal life in God's presence where full joy and pleasures never end (Ps. 16:11).

What God gave him in return was a gift that would be worth ten thousand blind lifetimes.

Let us be very careful in interpreting God's purposes in suffering—our own or someone else's. Often we cannot see any redeeming reason for it. It might appear or feel like God's judgment, or just the grinding gears of a blind, uncaring cosmos.

The man born blind reminds us that our perceptions and God's purposes can be very different, even opposite. If we are going to be skeptical, it's best to be skeptical of our perceptions. And he reminds us that when Jesus finally reveals the real purposes, we will find them more glorious than we ever dreamed and his reward so overwhelming that there will be no trace of bitterness, only overflowing gratitude.

That very day two of them were going to a village named Emmaus, about seven miles from Jerusalem, and they were talking with each other about all these things that had happened. While they were talking and discussing together, Jesus himself drew near and went with them. But their eyes were kept from recognizing him.

LUKE 24:13-16

27

THE EYES JESUS OPENED FIRST

CLEOPAS AND DISILLUSIONMENT

Luke 24:13–35

IT WAS SUNDAY AFTERNOON. Cleopas and his companion walked out Jerusalem's Western Gate and headed toward Emmaus. And they were clearly having an intense discussion.

About ten minutes into the journey, a stranger who had been walking near them suddenly asked, "What is this conversation that you are holding with each other as you walk?"

They just stopped and looked at him, dumbfounded. Jesus's execution was about the only thing anyone was talking about in Jerusalem. It had been the tragic climax to a week of controversy, confrontation, and political intrigue.

Perhaps "climax" was premature. A new twist had emerged that morning. Jesus's body was missing. No statements had been issued from the Sanhedrin or the Romans. There were rumors of a resurrection. The gossip mills were all running at full capacity.

Cleopas said, "Are you the only visitor to Jerusalem who does not know the things that have happened there in these days?"

The man replied, "What things?"

"Concerning Jesus of Nazareth, a man who was a prophet mighty in deed and word before God and all the people." Cleopas paused, clearly feeling this very deeply, then continued, "But we had hoped that he was the one to redeem Israel."

He quickly wiped his eyes and started walking again. "Yes, and besides all this, it is now the third day since these things happened. Moreover, some women of our company amazed us. They were at the tomb early in the morning, and when they did not find his body, they came back saying that they had even seen a vision of angels, who said that he was alive. Some of those who were with us went to the tomb and found it just as the women had said, but him they did not see."

They walked in silence for about a minute. Then the stranger said the last thing they expected: "O foolish ones, and slow of heart to believe all that the prophets have spoken!" Cleopas looked over at the stranger confused. Then the man looked right into Cleopas's eyes and said, "Was it not necessary that the Christ should suffer these things and enter into his glory?"

For the next two hours this mysterious man walked Cleopas and his friend through the entire Scriptures and explained all the references to the Christ. And as he did, the fire of their faith that had been extinguished on Golgotha flared back to life and burned with that familiar hope: their hope that Jesus was indeed the Christ. Could it really be true—Jesus resurrected?

And who was this man who so beautifully made sense of everything, and yet at first had seemed clueless? There was something peculiar about him . . . like they knew him from somewhere, but couldn't put their fingers on it.

The sun hung low in the sky ahead of them as they reached Emmaus. The stranger gave every indication that he intended to continue on. So the two revived disciples, almost desperately, pleaded with him to stay at least for the night. They were overjoyed when he agreed.

At dinner the man took some bread, pulled it apart, and gave them each a piece. As soon as the bread touched their hands they recognized who he was. Both gasped. And Jesus vanished.

○ ○

Why do you suppose these two men were "kept from recognizing" Jesus for hours? The clue, I believe, is in verse 25. Jesus called them "foolish" and "slow of heart to believe" the Scriptures. Their outward inability to recognize Jesus mirrored their inward unbelief of what the Scriptures revealed about him.

Now, Jesus fully intended to help them see him. But notice the priority of Jesus's revelation: before he opened their physical eyes, he purposed to open their heart-eyes. Why? Because it was of utmost importance to Jesus that these men "walk by faith, not by sight" (2 Cor. 5:7).

Jesus knew that between his resurrection and the full establishment of his kingdom would be the church age. His ascension was nearing. That meant these two men, all the other witnesses of his resurrection, and every generation of believers to come would not have his bodily presence for proof or guidance. They would have to rely on his "living and active" Word (Heb. 4:12) to "light [their] path" (Ps. 119:105). Post-ascension, Jesus would only be seen through the inerrant testimony recorded in the Scriptures and the imperfect testimony of followers whose heart-eyes were opened.

When God ordains things to happen contrary to our expectations (like Cleopas not expecting Jesus to die), those are times when we are tempted to doubt his Word—lose faith— and as a result lose sight of him. But not being able to see him doesn't mean that he isn't right there walking with us. We may simply not recognize him. Unbelief is blinding. Those are not the times to neglect his Word. Rather, that's when we really need it most.

It's when we really listen to Jesus that he will help us recognize him again.

"What I am doing you do not understand now, but afterward you will understand."

JOHN 13:7

28

"WHAT I AM DOING YOU DO NOT UNDERSTAND NOW"

PETER AND SANCTIFICATION

John 13:1–11

PETER WATCHED JESUS MAKE his way toward him, washing the feet of other disciples.

It had already been a confusing Passover. Jesus had been unusually burdened, close to tears all day. The atmosphere during the meal was charged with ominous anticipation.

Peter had grown used to Jesus doing and saying unpredictable things. But what Jesus was doing now was wrong. He was the last person in the room who should be washing feet.

All of Peter's life he had been taught that feet were dishonorable members of the body. They were usually dirty, frequently smelly, and among the most likely members to come in contact with things that the Law declared unclean.

Outside of immediate family, feet were washed by slaves and servants—ideally non-Jews so as not to subject any of the covenant people to such humiliation.

And one never insulted an honored person by pointing one's feet at them.

But here was the Messiah, the most honored Jew to ever walk the earth, stripped like a common slave with a towel around his waist willingly handling the unclean feet of his disciples. This was backwards. If anything, Peter should be down there washing Jesus's feet.

When Jesus got to Peter he smiled at him and reached for his feet. Peter pulled them back. "Lord, do you wash my feet?" (John 13:6).

Jesus loved Peter. The Rock never did anything, right or wrong, without jumping in with—or in this case withholding—both feet. He knew what Peter was thinking. So he replied, "What I am doing you do not understand now, but afterward you will understand" (v. 7).

Peter was simply unwilling to subject Jesus to such dishonor, so he said, "You shall never wash my feet" (v. 8).

Jesus's countenance became dead serious. "If I do not wash you, you have no share with me" (v. 8).

The shock of this statement stunned Peter for a second. He had been trying to preserve his Master's honor. But what Jesus was essentially telling him was, unless you let me bear your dishonor, your uncleanness, you can't be my disciple.

Well, he didn't understand what this all meant, but Peter would leave no doubt about his trust in and love for Jesus: "Lord, not my feet only but also my hands and my head!" (v. 9).

Joy radiated from Jesus's eyes and smile. And as he washed Peter's feet he said, "The one who has bathed does not need to wash, except for his feet, but is completely clean" (v. 10).

Then he paused for a moment and looked into Peter's eyes. This beloved man was unknowingly about to face the most difficult, grievous, and glorious three days of his life. He would benefit from this reassurance: "And you *are* clean."

Then his eyes dropped back to Peter's feet and he resumed washing. "But not every one of you" (v. 10).

Two observations from this story:

First, much of the Christian life is spent trusting Jesus now and understanding him later. Jesus typically does not feel it necessary to explain on the front end why he is doing something the way he is doing it. And like Peter, when it looks wrong to us, we are tempted to object to the Lord's will.

God understands and is patient with our confusion and even our deep wrestling or grief. But he wants us to trust him and not grumble or question in unbelief (Phil. 2:14). God's ways are not our ways (Isa. 55:8). His purposes for bringing, or not bringing, certain things to pass often extend far beyond us—maybe even generations beyond us.

So during those times we need to remember Jesus's words to Peter: "What I am doing you do not understand now, but afterward you will understand."

Second, what Jesus is bringing about in the sometimes confusing, sometimes very painful work he is doing in our lives is sanctification. He is washing our feet. He not only bathes us, completely removing the guilt of our sin in his cleansing work on the cross, but in love he keeps forgiving us (1 John 1:9) and disciplining us so that we will share his holiness (Heb. 12:10–11).

It is not as important to God that we understand his purposes in a particular providence as it is that we trust in his character. So together let's continue to "trust in the LORD with all [our] heart, and . . . not lean on [our] own understanding" (Prov. 3:5). Because one day, afterward, we will understand. And we will, with great joy, proclaim, "The LORD is righteous in all his ways and kind in all his works" (Ps. 145:17).

And Joseph's master took him and put him into the prison, the place where the king's prisoners were confined, and he was there in prison.

GENESIS 39:20

29

STAYING FAITHFUL WHEN THINGS GET WORSE

JOSEPH AND PERSEVERANCE

Sometime During Genesis 39:20–23

GENESIS CHAPTERS 37–41 TELL only the low and high points of Joseph's Egyptian slavery and imprisonment. But he spent at least twelve years there before he suddenly became the Egyptian Prime Minister. And during that terribly lonely, desolate time, things seemed to go from bad to worse. Imagine what Joseph might have experienced at about year nine into his sojourn.

○ ○

Darkness had swallowed the light again. Joseph dreaded the night in this foul Egyptian hellhole. It was hard to fight off the relentless hopelessness as he waited for the escape of sleep.

Day after monotonous day passed with no sign of change. The familiar desperation surged hot in his chest. His youth was seeping out the cracks of his cage. He was pacing in his soul. Joseph wanted to scream.

Fists to his forehead, he pleaded again with God in the dark for deliverance.

And he remembered. It was the remembering that kept his hope alive and bitterness at bay.

He rehearsed the stories of God that had filled him with awe as a child. God had promised Great-grandfather, Abraham, a child by his barren wife. But he made them wait an agonizing twenty-five years before giving them Grandfather Isaac. And God had promised Grandmother Rebekah that her older twin, Uncle Esau, would serve the younger twin, Father Jacob. But God had mysteriously woven human deception and immorality into his plan to make that happen.

Jacob's smile filled Joseph's mind. Oh Father! He covered his mouth to choke back his sobs. It had been nine years since he last saw that dear face. Would he ever see it again? Was Father still alive?

He felt something crawl across his leg. Leaping up, he brushed himself off. He shook out the mat. A shiver ran down his spine. Joseph hated spiders.

Lying back down he remembered how Father Jacob had been caught in his Uncle Laban's manipulative web for twenty long years. Yet God was faithful to his word and eventually delivered Jacob and brought him back to the Promised Land a wealthy man.

And then there were those strange dreams he had had. They had been unusually powerful, unlike any other dreams before or since. He felt ambivalent about them. They likely were the reason he was now in an Egyptian jail. His brothers' envy of his father's favor turned homicidal when he inferred that he had God's favor as well.

Distant screams let Joseph know another fight had broken out in the barracks. It made him grateful for his private cell, a favor bestowed when he became chief scribe to the warden.

He smiled at the irony of this "favor." Favor in a prison. His brothers would love this if they only knew. He seemed about as far away from what those dreams foretold as he could be.

Yet, as foolish as it seemed right now, Joseph could not shake the deep conviction that God meant to bring those dreams to pass. And he could not deny the strange pattern he saw in God's dealings with his forebears. God made stunning promises and then ordained time and circumstances to work in such ways as to make the promises seem impossible to fulfill. And then God moved.

The common thread Joseph traced through all the stories, the one thing God seemed to honor and bless more than anything else, was faith. Great-grandfather Abraham believed God's word. Grandfather Isaac believed God's word. Grandmother Rebekah believed God's word. Father Jacob believed God's word. They all believed even when it looked like God's word wasn't going to come true. And all of them ultimately saw God's faithfulness to his promises, despite circumstances and their own failings.

Faith-fueled peace doused the anxious fire in Joseph's chest. "I believe you, my God," he whispered. "Like my forefathers, I will wait for you. I have no idea what my being in an Egyptian prison has to do with your purposes. But I will keep honoring you here where you have placed me. Bring your word to pass as it seems best to you. I am yours. Use me!"

○ ○

In the biblical account it's tempting to see only Joseph's heroic character and achievements. But God does not want us to miss the largely silent, desperate years Joseph endured.

Imagine the pain of his brothers' betrayal, the separation from his father, the horror of slavery, the seduction and false accusation by Potiphar's wife, and the desperation he felt as his youth passed away in prison.

Sometimes faithfulness to God and his word sets us on a course where circumstances get worse, not better. It is then that knowing God's promises and his ways are crucial. Faith in God's future grace for us is what sustains us in those desperate moments.

We all love the fairytale ending of Joseph's story. And we should, because Joseph's life is a foreshadowing of a heavenly reality. God sent his Son to die and be raised in order to set his children "free indeed" (John 8:36). There is coming a day when those who are faithful, even to death (Rev. 2:10), will hear, "Well done, good and faithful servant. You have been faithful over a little; I will set you over much. Enter into the joy of your master" (Matt. 25:21).

Our current circumstances, however dismal or successful, are not our story's end. They are chapters in a much larger story that really does have a happily ever after.

One of the two who heard John speak and followed Jesus was Andrew, Simon Peter's brother.

JOHN 1:40

30

SERVE IN THE SHADOW GOD PLACES YOU

ANDREW AND HUMILITY

Various Texts

"ANDREW. OH! YOU'RE SIMON Peter's brother, aren't you?"

Andrew must have gotten used to that. Even the New Testament introduces him as "Andrew, Simon Peter's brother" (John 1:40). Peter's shadow is cast over Andrew from the beginning.

Andrew is mentioned by name twelve times in the New Testament. In ten of those he's named along with Peter, and usually as Peter's brother. Peter, on the other hand, has over one hundred and fifty mentions, and was a contributing author to the New Testament.

It's interesting to note that Andrew had the more impressive résumé to begin with. He had been a disciple of John the Baptist. So he brought more theological training and practical ministry experience to the team than Peter. Not only that, but he was one of Jesus's very first disciples (John 1:35–40). In fact, it was Andrew who went and "found his own brother Simon" and brought him to Jesus (John 1:41).

Yet even at this very first meeting it became clear that Jesus had plans concerning Simon that were different from Andrew.

Before Simon had said or done anything, Jesus gave him his new name of Cephas (Peter), the rock (John 1:42).

Peter was God's "workmanship, created in Christ Jesus for good works, which God prepared beforehand, that [he] should walk in them" (Eph. 2:10). We know of many of these good works because God gives them a lot of press.

But Andrew was equally God's workmanship. He too was created in Christ Jesus for good works that God had prepared beforehand. It's just that God chose not to give Andrew's works the same prominence he gave Peter's. And so Andrew served in Peter's shadow.

Did that ever bother him? Did he ever feel left out when Jesus included Peter in things like resurrecting the little girl (Mark 5:37) or the transfiguration (Matt. 17:1), but did not include him? Did he and Peter ever take walks together and talk about why brothers James and John seemed to function as one unit with Jesus, but not Peter and Andrew, at least not as much? We don't know. But considering the disciples' recurring debates over which one was the greatest (Mark 9:34), it's very feasible.

But Andrew had a great shadow-servant mentor in John the Baptist. Andrew had learned from John that "a person cannot receive even one thing unless it is given him from heaven" (John 3:27). John had seen Jesus's rise and his own decline in prominence and said with joy-filled faith, "He must increase, but I must decrease" (John 3:30).

And that is the cry of every true disciple. Following Jesus isn't about our prominence at all. It's about Jesus's prominence. Like the Twelve, we tend to lose sight of this easily.

When God gives one disciple five talents, another two talents, and another one talent, he has his reasons (Matt. 25:15). Very likely they are different from what we think (Isa. 55:9). But he knows what he's doing. We can trust him.

Today, be content with what you have (Heb. 13:5) and be faithful with what you have been given (Matt. 25:21). Humble yourself under God's mighty hand, trusting that he will exalt you at the proper time and in the proper way (1 Pet. 5:6).

Be like Andrew. This shadow-servant was faithful, obedient, responsive, trusted, willing, and courageous. Tradition says that he continued to preach the gospel and plant churches until he was martyred by crucifixion in the AD 60s.

Let us serve in the shadows God places us with that same humble, joy-filled, overcoming faith.

Now he was teaching in one of the synagogues on the Sabbath. And behold, there was a woman who had had a disabling spirit for eighteen years. She was bent over and could not fully straighten herself. When Jesus saw her, he called her over and said to her, "Woman, you are freed from your disability."

LUKE 13:10–12

31

THE DAY OF YOUR DELIVERANCE IS DECREED

DISABLED WOMAN AND SUFFERING

Luke 13:10–17

SHE HOBBLED INTO THE synagogue to hear the healing rabbi, hoping against hope. You see, she "had had a disabling spirit for eighteen years. She was bent over and could not fully straighten herself."

Eighteen years. How many of her tears had God collected in his bottle (Ps. 56:8)? How many of her prayers in his bowl (Rev. 5:8)?

Eighteen years of suffering. The slow burn of chronic pain had worn on her soul. She had suffered the loss of capacities she once took for granted. She had suffered the indignities of others' pity and disgust. She had suffered their suspicion that her body was bent under the weight of divine judgment.

Did she know that her affliction was satanic (v. 16)?

God knew. He knew all the ways she suffered, better than she did. And God had long permitted Satan to afflict her. Long, at least, for time-bound creatures whose mortal lives are measured in decades, not millennia (2 Pet. 3:8).

Why? We rarely are given answers to such questions.

But we get a rare answer in this woman's story. For suddenly, in that little synagogue, the grace of God engulfs her in the compassion of God the Son:

> When Jesus saw her, he called her over and said to her, "Woman, you are freed from your disability." And he laid his hands on her, and immediately she was made straight. (Luke 13:12–13)

Just like that. Eighteen years of bondage, and with a look, a word, and a touch the sea of her suffering parts. She has her exodus. This was the day God had decreed her deliverance.

All those weary years of grief just to find that her pain had been predestined to play a part in revealing Messiah to Israel. God had not been slow to show his compassion; he had been *patient* (2 Pet. 3:9). Was it worth it? "She glorified God" (v. 13).

Jesus's compassion and this woman's pain also had a far-reaching *purpose*. If you, like this woman, discovered that your seemingly meaningless affliction turned out to be infused with meaning beyond what you imagined possible and resulted in "joy that is inexpressible and filled with glory" (1 Pet. 1:8) for you and a multitude of others, would it be worth it? Sit down and catch your breath. It is. It's promised to you (2 Cor. 4:17).

And his compassion was *powerful*. When the synagogue ruler objected to such mercy as Sabbath-breaking, he found himself rebuked by the Lord of the Sabbath:

> "You hypocrites! Does not each of you on the Sabbath untie his ox or his donkey from the manger and lead it away to water it? And ought not this woman, a daughter of Abraham whom Satan bound for eighteen years, be loosed from this bond on the Sabbath day?" As he said these things, all his adversaries were put to shame, and all the people rejoiced at all the glorious things that were done by him. (Luke 13:15–17)

Not all the adversaries that were shamed were seen. Yes, the ruler of the synagogue and likely some Pharisees were humiliated. But Satan far more. This woman had been his captive, and he had been disarmed and overthrown with a compassionate word. A horrible harbinger of an approaching defeat he was fighting like hell to thwart.

And it was a holy harbinger of an approaching final deliverance for all who love the Lord's appearing:

> He will wipe away every tear from their eyes, and death shall be no more, neither shall there be mourning, nor crying, nor pain anymore, for the former things have passed away. (Rev. 21:4)

In this age, it is not the tears or mourning or crying or pain or death that is strange. "The whole world lies in the power of the evil one" (1 John 5:19). What's strange is their defeat.

Today you may say with Job, "My complaint is bitter; my hand is heavy on account of my groaning" (Job 23:2). You may say with Moses, "Return, O Lord! How long? Have pity on your servants! . . . Make us glad for as many days as you have afflicted us, and for as many years as we have seen evil" (Ps. 90:13–15).

But you need to know that, like this disabled woman, the patient, purposeful, powerful compassion of God in Christ for you is approaching like a relentless torrent. The day of your deliverance is decreed. It will come with a sudden joy. Every adversary will be shamed. Every tear will be wiped away. And the days he will make you glad will drown the days you have seen evil into glorious and happy oblivion (Rom. 8:18).

When two years had elapsed, Felix was succeeded by Porcius Festus. And desiring to do the Jews a favor, Felix left Paul in prison.

ACTS 24:27

32

HAS JESUS BEEN WORTH IT?

PAUL AND CHRISTIAN HEDONISM

Sometime During Acts 24–25

○ ○

BENEATH INTELLECTUAL OBJECTIONS TO Jesus's claims are often deep-seated fears. Imagine a conversation between Paul and "Jonathan," a friend from Paul's pre-Christian days who visits the old apostle during his two-year stay in Felix's Caesarean prison.

○ ○

Jonathan was escorted into the dingy cell where his old friend looked up at him from a small table covered in parchments. The close air smelled of mold. Jonathan tried not to look shocked.

Paul looked puzzled for moment and then his eyes went wide with recognition. "Jonathan?" He hurried stiffly around the table to embrace his friend. Saul smelled worse than the mold, Jonathan thought.

"Here," Paul said as he cleared more parchments from a chair and pulled it over. "Sit down!"

As he did, Jonathan said, "So, is this your idea of a Mediterranean holiday?" Paul laughed. It was the same loud, healthy laugh Jonathan remembered. He missed it.

"Welcome to Caesarea Maritima, the jewel of Palestine! My

villa, however, is less than luxurious." The two smiled word-lessly for a moment. Then Paul said, "It is so good to see you again, Jonathan."

"Look at you, Saul. You're an old man before your time. You walk like my father." Paul laughed again. He had always liked Jonathan's candor.

"Where'd you get that ugly scar above your eye?" Jonathan asked. Paul answered, "I took a stone to the head in Lystra."[1]

"You were stoned?" Jonathan exclaimed. "Saul! What happened to you?"

"Well, after the priest of Zeus had wanted . . ."

"No, I don't mean why you were *stoned*. I can guess that. I need to know what happened to *you*. We haven't spoken for over twenty-five years." Jonathan's eyes misted. "But we once were friends. You were among my closest. Some of my best memories are the hours we spent debating Mishnah and politics."

"Which I always won!"

"Yes, even when you didn't!" Both men laughed. The old joke eased the awkwardness.

"The last time you and I were together like this was just after the Council granted you the commission to Damascus. Remember? You were so angry over the Nazarene sect. I tried to get you to take Gamaliel's approach.[2] But you were immovable. 'We cannot just let this poison spread!' you told me. Then the next thing I know a plot is being formed to kill you because *you're* spreading the poison in Damascus!"

"Do you know what happened to me?" asked Paul. "Of course," said Jonathan. "Your story is notorious. But, Saul . . . *this*?" Jonathan gestured around the cell.

"What?" Paul's eyes pierced with his familiar intensity.

"This doesn't strike you as a bit crazy? You would have

[1] See Acts 14:19–23.
[2] See Acts 5:34–39.

become a leader of the Sanhedrin. But instead you've spent decades wandering the Empire half zealot, half fugitive preaching Jesus like a madman. And it's cost you *everything*. You lost your faith. You lost a promising career. You lost your friends. You've lost your youth. You have no family, no home, no money. Now you're a prisoner of Rome, Saul! And if you ever go back Jerusalem, you're a dead man. Your life looks like a tragic waste.

"That's why I've come. Before you're . . . gone, I need to ask: has Jesus been worth it, Saul?"

Paul prayed silently then answered, "My life has been a tragic waste—*if* Jesus was not raised from the dead. If Jesus's body was stolen as your Council claims, I am a fool—among men most to be pitied (1 Cor. 15:19).

"But, Jonathan, if Jesus *was* raised, then what? Then my faith was not lost but found. Then my career has been wonderful. Then I have family and friends all over Asia Minor. If Jesus was raised, if I'm doing his will, if he's providing all I really need and guiding me safely to his heavenly kingdom, what need do I have of money or houses or freedom?

"So the real question is, was Jesus raised from the dead, Jonathan? The answer determines whether I'm wasting my life in a Roman prison or you are wasting yours in respectable Jewish society."

Jonathan was quiet for a minute, and then sighed, "I don't know. The body-theft story grows weaker with time. I can't see why Jesus's disciples would suffer so much over a lie for so little profit. Then there are the miracles. And there's *you*. I don't know what to do with your life. You believe in Jesus in a way I have never believed in Judaism. But, Saul, honestly, I fear to examine your question too hard. If I begin to believe in Jesus's resurrection I'll lose everything. That scares me. I don't think I could do . . . *this*." He gestured at the cell again.

Paul's eyes were soft and his words hard. "Then, Jonathan,

you care less for God and truth than for security and comfort. Your fear of losing them powers your unbelief. Jesus once said, 'Whoever would save his life will lose it, but whoever loses his life for my sake will find it. For what will it profit a man if he gains the whole world and forfeits his soul?' (Matt. 16:25–26). So I need to ask you: is security and comfort worth *that*, Jonathan?

"Stop looking at what you would *lose* if Jesus was raised from the dead, and start looking at what you would *gain!*" Paul's haggard face became radiant. "I'll answer your question: yes! Jonathan, Jesus has been far more than worth it! Everything I've lost is like rubbish compared to gaining him (Phil. 3:8)! Come and see!"

○ ○

The freedom to follow Jesus comes from seeing the reward. If we see it, the costs cease to be costly.

> And without faith it is impossible to please him, for whoever would draw near to God must believe that he exists and that he rewards those who seek him. (Heb. 11:6)

While [Pilate] was sitting on the judgment seat, his wife sent word to him, "Have nothing to do with that righteous man, for I have suffered much because of him today in a dream."

MATTHEW 27:19

33

POWERFUL, PRAGMATIC PAWN OF PROVIDENCE

PONTIUS PILATE AND GOVERNING AUTHORITIES

Sunday Morning, Following the
Events of John 18-19

PONTIUS PILATE IS A picture of worldly power. He is competent and calculating, he is pragmatic and self-preserving. But for all his shrewdness, his life demonstrates that the "Word above all earthly powers, no thanks to them, abideth."[1]

Imagine a conversation over breakfast between Pilate and his wife, Procula,[2] on the Sunday morning following Jesus's crucifixion, just before they receive word that the tomb is empty.

∘∘

"You're quiet again this morning, Procula. Still brooding over the Galilean?"

"I can't shake this ominous feeling that something is going to happen because he was executed. My dream was so disturbing, so vivid."

"Well, I can't govern by the superstitious dreams of women."

---

[1] From Martin Luther's hymn, "A Mighty Fortress Is Our God," 1529.
[2] Matthew 27:19 is the only reference to Pilate's wife in the New Testament. Christian traditions have named her either Procula or Claudia.

"He was a righteous man. You should not have sentenced him to death."

"I didn't sentence him! The Sanhedrin sentenced him!"

"You pronounced the judgment."

"Yes, and I didn't have a choice, Procula! We've been over this. He broke a Jewish blasphemy law, they wanted him dead, they used me to do it. I did everything in my power to release him!"

Procula was soft-spoken in her persistence. "It was in your power to release him."

Pilate pressed his palm against his forehead and clenched his jaw, suppressing his volatile temper.

"You know what I mean! I told them three times that I found no guilt in him. I tried to pass him off to Herod. I tried scourging him to pacify them. Nothing. They were dead set. I even gave the crowd a choice between releasing a convicted murderer or Jesus, and whom did they choose? The murderer!"

Looking up at his wife Pilate said with exasperation, "What did you expect me to do?"

"Not condemn the righteous. Aren't you supposed to administer justice from Rome's tribunal?"

"No! *I'm* supposed to make sure that Judea poses no problems for Tiberius!"

"Even if that means ignoring the truth?"

"Truth," Pilate scoffed. "Whose truth, Procula? The Sanhedrin's? Tiberius's? Your dream's? The Galilean's? Truth is what got the Galilean killed. I gave him every chance to refute the accusations, but you know what he said to me? 'For this purpose I have come into the world—to bear witness to the truth' (John 18:37). And you know what his truth was? That he was a king of some kingdom outside of this world. Well, apparently the Sanhedrin seemed to think that his truth was a dangerous lie."

"Do you think he was dangerous?"

Pilate sighed and sipped his wine. "I don't know. He wasn't like the Zionist zealots. There was no diatribe against Rome. He hardly said anything. He didn't even seem angry. If he threatened anyone I think it was the Sanhedrin. I know a set-up when I see one. A midnight trial, a demand for immediate crucifixion. This wasn't about their holy law. It was about power. Caiaphas was getting rid of a problem."

"Were you getting rid of a problem?"

Pilate's eyes flashed with anger. "Believe me, Procula, I have bigger problems than Jesus to worry about. My problem is Caesar. That mob would have turned into a riot if I had released Jesus. Riots in Jerusalem always lead to some Jew getting killed, and I can't risk any more Jewish blood on my hands right now without inviting Tiberius's inquiry.

"And then I had the chief priests suddenly feigning loyalty to Caesar and publicly questioning mine. If I had released him, can you imagine their glee at reporting to Tiberius that I was unwilling to deal with a rival to Caesar? When all was said and done, my choice was between Caesar and a delusional Galilean. That choice was obvious to me."

At that moment a servant stepped into the room. "What is it?" Pilate asked.

"Marcus Antonius is requesting to see you, sir."

"Marcus? This early in the morning? That can't be good. Send him in."

The young officer strode in.

"What is it, Marcus?"

"The Galilean, sir. He's disappeared."

○ ○

Pilate was a man of pragmatic worldly wisdom. He probably saw himself as a realist. Which was ironic, because he got reality dead wrong. He seemed to see Jesus as a disposable pawn in a political chess game, when in reality he himself was the pawn and Jesus the King.

And this is crucial to remember when, for Jesus's sake, we find ourselves at the mercies of powerful earthly authorities (governing, vocational, familial, or religious) that "seek their own interests, not those of Jesus Christ" (Phil. 2:21). Their selfish interests may even inflict evil upon us. But the Bible is clear: what they mean for evil, God means, and will turn, for our good (Gen. 50:20).

Remember Jesus's word to Pilate: "You would have no authority over me at all unless it had been given you from above" (John 19:11). The same is true of us. Those in authority over us are there by God's decree, and they will give an account to him.

But for us "neither death nor life, nor angels nor rulers, nor things present nor things to come, *nor powers*, nor height nor depth, nor anything else in all creation, will be able to separate us from the love of God in Christ Jesus our Lord" (Rom. 8:38–39).

After this he went out and saw a tax collector named Levi, sitting at the tax booth. And he said to him, "Follow me." And leaving everything, he rose and followed him.

LUKE 5:27-28

34

"FOLLOW ME"

LEVI AND GRACE

Luke 5:27–32; Matthew 9:9–13; Mark 2:13–17

THE ONLY THING THAT qualifies us to be followers of Jesus is that we are sinners who need grace. Sinners are the only kind of people Jesus calls, as the apostle Levi (Matthew) discovered.

○ ○

Levi looked around the campfire circle at Jesus and the other eleven disciples. Strange rabbinical school, he thought. Not exactly the cream of the scholarly crop. This rabbi with no formal theological training had a motley crew of disciples that tended to be a bit heavy on fishermen.

But he saw himself as the oddest of the oddballs.

Levi had been a tax collector. That meant he had essentially worked for Rome. And that meant he had been considered a traitor by most of his neighbors. "Tax collectors and sinners" were synonyms.

Whatever Roman official had crafted the empire's internal revenue system had been a genius. It was designed to encourage collection corruption. So long as Rome received its prescribed amount from a region, collectors were free to keep any overage. There was serious money to be made by the financially ambitious, and ethically . . . unprincipled. And the more corrupt the collector, the more alienated he became from his own people, and thus increasingly dependent on Rome's continued governance.

It had been a hard vocational choice. A tax collector's income was both sizable and reliable. It wasn't as vulnerable as other trades to the fluctuations of the local market or the caprice of rain clouds. But it required that one be willing to endure a different kind of drought: social respect. When Levi became a collector, he knew he was trading his reputation for financial security. Thereafter he had kept a prudent distance from synagogue society and made his friends within the "sinner" caste.

And then came the strangest and best day of his life.

Levi had heard about Rabbi Jesus. Everyone seemed to be talking about him. There were reports of astounding miracles. People were puzzling over his parables.

And now Jesus had come to town! Levi had hoped to hear him preach, but he was swamped with work. Tax collectors dare not disappoint their regional managers.

Sitting in his tax booth Levi had seen a bustling crowd approaching. Experience had taught him to keep his head down and look busy to avoid making eye contact with his despisers.

But the bustle had stopped right in front of him. He could feel peoples' eyes on him. He heard the hiss of many whispers. He looked up cautiously. An intense young man was staring at him. He knew immediately it was Jesus.

A nervous knot formed in his stomach. He braced for a rabbinical rebuke.

But what Jesus said was, "Follow me." There were gasps from the crowd and the hissing turned to a hum of collective shock. Levi sat in a frozen stun. Jesus was clearly speaking to *him*. But what did he mean?

Jesus's expression grew more earnest and he beckoned with his hand. He wanted Levi to literally follow him—at that very moment!

A jumble of thoughts crashed around in Levi's mind. What about the tax booth? All these records . . . Where was Jesus going? Would they be gone long? But clarity immediately began to swallow up this confusion: Jesus meant give it all up and follow him. Jesus wanted him for a disciple.

Jesus wants *me*? Does he know . . . Then suddenly he knew that Jesus *knew*.

He was filled with an exhilaration and joy he had never experienced before. For so long he had assumed (and been told) that God didn't want anything to do with him. But now it seemed that, through Jesus, God was speaking directly to him. And despite the fact that abandoning his booth would certainly cost him his job, Levi shocked himself with the deep desire to gladly trade financial security for following Jesus—this rabbi he didn't even know. It was both inexplicable and irresistible.

So he laid down his quill, stood up, and simply fell in behind Jesus. He had never felt more free in his life.

Now, sitting around the evening fire a year later, it hit Levi all over again how strange and wonderful and merciful are the ways of God. Who would have guessed that he would pluck a tax collector, of all people, right out of his booth and appoint him to be a disciple of Israel's long-awaited Messiah? And now many tax collectors and sinners were swelling Jesus's ranks.

○○

Being a sinner was the only qualification Levi had for joining Jesus's disciple band. Jesus had come to call sinners to repentance (Luke 5:32). Levi was sick with the disease of sin, and Jesus, the Great Physician, healed him (Luke 5:31).

Because of that, Levi later threw a party at his house and invited his sinner friends to meet Jesus. And many followed him (Mark 2:15).

Jesus did not call us because of our righteousness or gifting. He called us when we were dead in our sins (Eph. 2:1) and blinded by the god of this world (2 Cor. 4:4). He called us when all we had was need.

And now that we are his disciples, all we redeemed sinners still really have is our need of him. He is the Vine and we are branches; apart from him, we can do nothing (John 15:5). He supplies us with the Spirit (Gal. 3:5) so that we serve only in the strength and grace that he supplies (1 Pet. 4:11).

> For by grace you have been saved through faith. And this is not your own doing; it is the gift of God, not a result of works, so that no one may boast. For we are his workmanship, created in Christ Jesus for good works, which God prepared beforehand, that we should walk in them. (Eph. 2:8–10)

We never stop following Jesus. Every day is a new invitation to believe in, rejoice in, and respond to his inexplicable and irresistible invitation.

"Return to your home, and declare how much God has done for you."

LUKE 8:39

35

WHEN FOLLOWING JESUS MEANS GOING HOME

THE GADARENE AND APPOINTMENT

Luke 8:26–39

WE TEND TO THINK of following Jesus as leaving behind the familiar for the unfamiliar. But sometimes, like the Gadarene Demoniac, the more difficult call is to go back home.

○ ○

For the first time in a long time he was in full control of his mind. He could think! No rage. No fear. No torment. Peace, like the quiet sea. He actually wanted to keep his clothes on.

But the most strangely wonderful thing of all was his sense of cleanness. His soul was clean.

The tomb-man from Gadara looked up at Jesus again. His lucid mind mulled over the words "Son of the Most High God."

Who would have thought that the Son of God looked so much like other Jewish men? He wasn't very big and not especially distinctive. The tomb-man had beaten off much more impressive-looking men in his demonic rages.

It was, in fact, his demons that had recognized Jesus. "Son of God" was their term. What was it that *they* saw? In all his tormented years, he had never felt anything like the terror that coursed through him when he saw Jesus get out of the boat. It was the terror of the damned. He had thought he'd been living in hell already. Now he knew better.

And now, with the demons gone, nothing he had ever experienced came close to the safety and peace he felt simply being near Jesus. He had only known Jesus for a few hours, but he had already determined to be Jesus's disciple for life. Life with him would be heaven on earth.

The man looked out on the Tiberias. Pig carcasses were washing ashore and drifting out to sea. He shivered at the disturbing memory. He felt Jesus's reassuring hand on his shoulder.

A noise made them all turn back toward the hill. A small crowd of people was approaching, and the pig herdsmen were leading the way. He could hear alarm in their voices.

A few men went on to survey the dead floating herd. But the rest stopped some twenty feet away. Everyone strained for a look at the tomb-man. He recognized most of them.

He was used to seeing fear in their eyes. But it was different this time. As a herdsman recounted what happened, they kept looking at him and then to Jesus. It was Jesus they were afraid of.

The crowd's murmuring crescendoed into anxious pleas: "Please leave! We don't want any more trouble here!" Some were already hurrying back toward the city. For years the tomb-man, this one-man barracks of a thousand devils, had terrorized them. And now here was someone even more powerful. Whatever witchcraft Jesus possessed, they wanted it far away from them.

The tomb-man felt confusion and grief. They didn't understand! Jesus wasn't anything like the demons. Jesus's power was clean, holy. Jesus was potently kind. They were jumping to the wrong conclusions. If they would just listen to what he had to say . . .

But Jesus motioned to Peter to ready the boat. He was leaving! He wasn't even going to explain himself.

The man jumped up and said to him, "Sir, please, please may I go with you? I'll follow you anywhere! I'll do anything!"

Jesus looked intensely at him for a moment without speaking. Then he put his reassuring hand on the man's shoulder again and said, "Return to your home, and declare how much God has done for you."

○ ○

The words "return to your home" must have made this man's heart sink. Home for him was not a warm place of sentimental memories. Home was a place of memories so dark and full of pain that he likely just wanted to escape them and never go back.

But sometimes following Jesus means being sent back to a place where we once knew desolation and indescribable anguish. The thought of returning there conjures up fear of our old demons and the people who knew us as we were back then. But Jesus sends us back because it is there that the grace of God in our lives will shine the brightest.

What Jesus wants us to know is that his salvation and his protection extend to those old, horrible haunts. If he can break the death grip Satan once had on us and set us free, then he can redeem the places of our former slavery and make them showcases of God's omnipotent grace.

Do not be afraid. The Good Shepherd will walk with you and protect you on the darkest road (Ps. 23:4). Declare how much God has done for you. You are being sent because there are other tomb-people to free.

❄ desiringGod

If you would like to explore further the vision of God and life presented in this book, we at Desiring God would love to serve you. We have thousands of resources to help you grow in your passion for Jesus Christ and help you spread that passion to others. At our website, www.desiringGod.org, you'll find almost everything John Piper has written and preached, including more than forty books. We've made over thirty years of his sermons available free online for you to read, listen to, download, and in some cases watch.

In addition, you can access hundreds of articles, find out where John Piper is speaking, learn about our conferences, and browse our online store. John Piper receives no royalties from the books he writes and no compensation from Desiring God. The funds are all reinvested into our gospel-spreading efforts. Desiring God also has a whatever-you-can-afford policy, designed for individuals with limited discretionary funds. If you'd like more information about this policy, please contact us at the address or phone number below. We exist to help you treasure Jesus Christ and his gospel above all things because he is most glorified in you when you are most satisfied in him. Let us know how we can serve you!

Desiring God
Post Office Box 2901 Minneapolis, Minnesota 55402
888.346.4700   mail@desiringGod.org

GENERAL INDEX

SCRIPTURE INDEX